Books by Albert Marrin

The Airman's War
Overlord
Victory in the Pacific
The Sea Rovers
War Clouds in the West
1812: The War Nobody Won

1812

THE WAR
NOBODY WON

1812

THE WAR NOBODY WON

Albert Marrin

ILLUSTRATED WITH
Old Prints & Engravings,
and Diagrams & Maps
by Patricia A. Tobin

ATHENEUM · 1985 · NEW YORK

LIBRARY OF CONGRESS CATALOGING IN PUBLICATION DATA

Marrin, Albert.   1812: the war nobody won.

"Illustrated with photos and prints."
Bibliography: p. 169.
Includes index.
SUMMARY: Describes the causes and leading events
of the early nineteenth-century conflict
between Great Britain and the United States.
1. United States — History — War of 1812 — Juvenile literature.
[1. United States — History — War of 1812]
I. Title.
E354.M27   1985   973.5'2   84-21623
ISBN 0-689-31075-7

Published simultaneously in Canada by
McClelland & Stewart, Ltd.
Composition by Maryland Linotype, Baltimore, Maryland
Printed and bound by Fairfield Graphics,
Fairfield, Pennsylvania
Designed by Marilyn Marcus
First Edition

For Stacey and Wendy

Contents

I don't like Americans; I never did, and never shall like them. . . . I have no wish to eat with them, drink with them, deal with or consort with them in any way; but let me tell the whole truth, *nor* fight with them, were it not for the laurels to be acquired, by overcoming an enemy so brave, determined, and alert, and in every way so worthy of one's steel, as they have always proved.

—Lieutenant Michael Scott, Royal Navy, 1829

1812

THE WAR
NOBODY WON

1

The Second War with Great Britain

Two o'clock, the afternoon of June 22, 1807. A gleaming summer's day with fleecy clouds drifting across the blue sky. The sea calm, long low swells reaching toward the eastern horizon.

The U.S.S. *Chesapeake*, Captain James Barron commanding, had just left the safety of Chesapeake Bay and set out across the Atlantic Ocean bound for Europe. This was no leisurely cruise, for the warship was behind schedule. Many things that should have been done in port were left to be attended to while at sea.

Sailors, barefooted, sweat streaming down their backs, went about their tasks. The deck was cluttered with coils of rope and cabin furniture, duffel bags and flour barrels, chicken coops and biscuit boxes, each needing to be stowed in its proper place. And somewhere under this clutter — no one knew exactly where — lay the rope matches and horns of fine black powder for the thirty-eight cannon that lined the gun deck.

The Virginia coast was fading into the distance when a hoarse cry came from high in the ship's rigging. "Sail ho-o-o! Sail to starboard!" a lookout shouted. Men strained their eyes and began to point with outstretched arms. There, about thirty miles ahead and to starboard (to the right), another vessel was making way under a full spread of canvas. By her lines and the shape of her sails, she, too, seemed like a warship.

After about an hour the stranger lowered her topsails, allowing *Chesapeake* to catch up until they were in calling distance. She was H.M.S. *Leopard*, fifty guns, and Captain Humphreys, her commander, had important letters for Europe. Since carrying another ship's mail was a courtesy of the sea, Captain Barron slowed down while *Leopard* sent a longboat alongside.

Soon a young British lieutenant was being shown into the captain's cabin. No, he had no letters for Europe, only an order to search American ships for deserters from the Royal Navy.

Barron was stunned when he learned of the lieutenant's mission. "Sir!" he said in a voice choking with emotion, "this is a national vessel of the United States." No one would be allowed to search the ship or question its crew about anything. After sending the lieutenant on his way, he ordered the crew to battle stations. But since the equipment to work the guns couldn't be found, *Chesapeake* was like a toothless shark waiting for the enemy to strike.

He struck — hard. *Leopard*'s gun ports opened, revealing long, black cannon, their muzzles painted bright red, like so many gaping mouths. One of the guns belched fire, sending a shot across *Chesapeake*'s bow, the signal to surrender or be destroyed. The British gunners then cut loose with everything they had. Again and again all the cannon on one side of their ship, or broadside, sent iron balls crashing into the defenseless vessel. She trembled under their impact, which knocked men off their feet and sent them sprawling across the deck. The Americans could return only one shot, fired when an officer grabbed a hot coal from the cooking fire with his bare hands and held it to the touchhole of a cannon.

An old broadside with a poem decrying the evils of the British
impressment of American sailors, one of the causes of the War of 1812.

A few minutes later, with twenty-one dead and wounded,
Barron hauled down Old Glory rather than see his crew
massacred.

The British lieutenant returned this time with a detach-
ment of grim-faced marines. *Chesapeake*'s crew was then
lined up on deck and he went down the line scanning the

sullen, fidgeting men. Four sailors, including a free Negro from Philadelphia, were picked out as deserters. Despite protests that they were United States citizens, the marines hustled them aboard *Leopard* at gunpoint. Three were later whipped and sent to duty on British warships, while the fourth was hung from the highest mast of a man-of-war. Captain Barron was allowed to return to port with his battered vessel.

This wasn't the first time that Americans had been roughly handled by the British at sea, nor would it be the last. For the United States of 1807 was not a world power; indeed, she hadn't even celebrated her twenty-fifth birthday as an independent country. Her army was small. Her navy was tiny. And, weak as she was, she found herself caught in the middle of a battle of giants.

The battling giants were Great Britain and France. Some years earlier, the French had a revolution in which Napoleon Bonaparte came to power. Napoleon was not only a dictator, but one of the greatest generals of all time. Wherever he led his armies, they were victorious, defeating one powerful nation after another.

In 1807, as in 1940, when Adolf Hitler seemed unbeatable, only Great Britain held out while Western Europe lay under Napoleon's heel. Britain survived because she was protected by her floating walls of wood, by the Royal Navy. Napoleon might command vast armies, but he couldn't command them to walk on water. The Island Kingdom remained safe only as long as it controlled the surrounding seas.

Never once did the Royal Navy lose a major battle to the French. In October, 1805, the opposing fleets met near Cape Trafalgar off Spain's southeastern coast for a tremendous battle. As the ships drew near, Admiral Lord Horatio Nelson signaled from his flagship, "England expects every man to do his duty." Although Nelson received his death wound that day, he lived long enough to hear that he had won the battle and saved his country from invasion.

It was easier for an admiral and a nobleman like Nelson to do his duty than for his sailors to do theirs. Life for the ordinary seaman in the Royal Navy was dull, dirty, and

War with the French dictator Napoleon brought Great Britain into conflict with American rights as a neutral in the struggle.

deadly. Voyages seemed endless, many crews never setting foot on land for three years at a time. When not dodging French cannonballs, sailors were busy keeping their ships shipshape. They were forever hauling on ropes, mending sails and holystoning, scrubbing the decks with salt water.

Although exhausted from the day's work, sailors seldom enjoyed a full night's sleep. The bosun's whistle constantly shrieked through the darkness, rousing them for some drill or special duty. In the morning, the last man out was whipped until he bled.

"All hands stand by to witness punishment" was an order often heard in the ships of His Majesty King George III. British seamen were always being whipped, since whipping, and the hangman's noose, were thought necessary for discipline. Most offenses were punished by sixty lashes on the bare back with the "cat," or cat-of-nine-tails, a whip made of nine strands of braided rope knotted at the ends. Salt was then rubbed into the raw wounds, a pail of water emptied over the sailor's head, and he was returned to duty.

Flogging aboard a British vessel.

Serious rule-breaking meant "flogging through the fleet," as savage a punishment as can be imagined. The offender was brought to a longboat and tied to a triangle-shaped rack. The boat was then rowed to each ship in the fleet and, as drums beat and everyone watched, he was whipped, usually for a grand total of five hundred lashes. Many died during the ordeal. Those who survived could never be the same men again, most being crippled for life or driven insane by pain.

Sailors' food could be as deadly as the discipline. Meat, when available, was nearly always rotten and covered with purply-black mold. Ship's biscuit, a type of bread baked hard as rock, was home to an interesting assortment of creatures. Before eating, it was wise to tap the biscuits on the table to shake some of the maggots, mites, and beetles out of their burrows. Sailors often ate biscuits in dark corners so as not to see what was going into their mouths. Biscuits were washed down with water so green and slimy that men held their noses while drinking. Eleven-year-old Bernard Cole-ridge, who served as a cabin boy aboard a warship, wrote to his parents:

> We live on beef which has been near ten or eleven years in corn (brine) and on biscuit which quite makes your throat cold in eating it owing to the maggots which are very cold when you eat them, like calves-foot jelly . . . being very fat indeed. . . . We drink water of the color of the bark of a pear-tree with plenty of little maggots and weavils in it and wine which is exactly like bullock's (bull's) blood and saw-dust mixed together.

The only relief from this diet was a daily ration of grog, or watered-down rum mixed with sugar and lemon juice. The idea was to save your ration for a few days, or get a shipmate to give you his. A double or triple dose would get you "groggy," drunk enough to forget your troubles for a while. But if you were caught — sixty lashes with the cat. No wonder upwards of two thousand men deserted the Royal Navy every year. Since Europe was at war, deserters usually signed up with American merchant ships or joined the United States Navy.

Most deserters preferred merchant vessels, however. The pay was good — ten times better than in British ships. The food, though not fancy, was good stick-to-your-ribs fare. American seamen ate salt pork and beef washed down with tankards of beer. They also enjoyed a boiled oatmeal soup called "burgoo" and "plum duff," a tasty mixture of flour and raisins. Best of all, they were treated as human beings. American sea captains couldn't order more than twelve lashes even for serious offenses.

His Majesty's officers did everything possible to bring back deserters. Forcing ships' crews to watch a flogging around the fleet or a hanging was meant to discourage others from escaping. Punishment, they believed, had to be cruel to be effective. For if deserters were allowed to get away easily, Britain would lose her first line of defense against Napoleon.

Bringing back deserters meant stopping and searching American ships. But how do you tell an Englishman from an American? In the early 1800s, when most American families originally came from the British Isles, both peoples looked pretty much alike and spoke the same way. Free Negroes, moreover, served in the ships of both nations.

It was natural, then, that British boarding parties should mistake American citizens for deserters. Even when they found a real deserter, he had often become a naturalized American, claiming protection under his new flag.

British commanders also used the search for deserters as an excuse for *impressment*. According to their country's law, the captain of a warship that was undermanned could stop any British merchantman on the high seas to impress, or force, the needed sailors into his crew. The strongest and most skilled sailors were taken, leaving the merchant captain often with less than half his crew after a visit from the Royal Navy.

If no British ships were sighted, an American vessel would do just as well. Backed by a squad of marines, an officer could call anyone he pleased a deserter. A sailor might be taken even if his papers showed that he had been a United States citizen for twenty years, because the British claimed that no one born in their country could ever give up his citizenship. "Once an Englishman always an Englishman" wasn't just a saying, but a rule enforced with gunpowder and iron.

Americans dreaded impressment. Stories were told in Yankee seaports of men who jumped overboard and drowned rather than go aboard a British man-of-war. One sailor asked to go below to pack his duffel bag and chopped off his left hand so as not to be taken. Still, between 1793 and 1812, over fifteen thousand Americans were impressed, enough to man the United States Navy of the day three times over.

American trade also suffered because of the war in Europe. Britain and France fought not only on the battlefield, but by trying to destroy each other's ability to make war. Beginning in 1806, Britain clamped a blockade around mainland Europe. His Majesty's Government issued a series of Orders in Council declaring that no nation could sell goods useful for war to France, her colonies, or the countries under her control. But since anything, including food, can be useful in war, Britain was really cutting off any trade with Europe. Napoleon then struck back with orders blockading the British Isles.

The United States was in a no-win situation. Since Europe was the chief customer for American-made goods and farm products, our merchants were bound to offend one side or the other. People could only nod in agreement when Thomas Jefferson, the president from 1801 to 1809, said that "England has become a den of pirates and France has become a den of thieves." Each country captured American ships, claiming they were trading with the enemy.

But British actions were the most resented. After the Battle of Trafalgar, France lacked the ships to keep up a really tight blockade. Britain's naval strength, however, grew daily. And Americans saw that strength in action every day. It is hard to catch ships on the open ocean and search their cargoes as they roll with the great swells. It is much easier to wait outside harbors and stop them as they come and go. Thus every American seaport was shadowed by British warships. No merchantman moved through its entrance without being stopped and searched. If French-made goods, or goods bound for France, were found, ship and cargo were sold at the British naval base of Halifax, Nova Scotia, in Canada, and the "prize" money shared by the warship's crew.

Stopping American ships on their own coasts was bad enough, but the Royal Navy went further. If a warship needed food or other supplies, the captain sent marines to get them from the nearest town. Note: we said *get*, not *buy*. If the Americans refused to give up their goods, the warship came within range of the town and opened its gun ports to underline the "request."

The United States Government protested against these unfriendly acts. The president called in the British ambassador. The secretary of state wrote to the British cabinet. The American ambassador in London met with the prime minister. The result of all this calling and writing and meeting was exactly nothing. Although His Majesty's Government was sorry that innocent Americans were harmed, it insisted that the Royal Navy would go on searching and seizing and impressing whenever and wherever it pleased.

In truth, Great Britain had no fear of offending the United States. Many Englishmen still thought of Americans as half-civilized yokels who could be pushed around. They hadn't forgiven them for the Revolution, which, they claimed, the colonists had won because they were lucky. Benjamin Franklin understood this when he said, "the War of the Revolution has been won, but the War of Independence is still to be fought." Franklin understood that the young nation would have to fight another war to convince Great Britain that the Revolution wasn't a mistake and to win her respect.

War fever spread through the United States in the wake of the *Chesapeake* affair. People were furious, demanding war in revenge for the insult to the flag. President Jefferson, however, had other ideas. For war meant bloodshed and destruction, which were to be avoided as long as there was any chance of settling differences peacefully. Jefferson believed that economic pressure rather than military force would bring Great Britain and France to their senses. Since

President Thomas Jefferson tried to make the British and French respect American rights at sea by cutting off the nation's trade with the whole world.

both sides were eager for American trade, he decided to cut off trade until they promised to respect our rights. Thus, late in 1807, Congress passed an Embargo Act halting trade with the whole world. No American vessel was permitted to sail the high seas. No European vessel could bring goods to, or carry them away from, our seaports.

The Embargo Act caused more suffering at home than in Europe. Hundreds of ships rotted at dockside. Thousands of honest seafaring men lost their jobs. Businessmen went bankrupt, losing their life's savings. At last Jefferson had to admit failure. Just before leaving the presidency in March, 1809, he signed a law repealing the embargo. It was replaced by the Non-Intercourse Act, which allowed Americans to trade with all nations except Great Britain and France. The act offered to reopen trade with these countries the moment they stopped interfering with American ships.

Jefferson was followed in office by James Madison, a friend he loved as a son. A small, quiet man who seldom smiled in public, President Madison seemed cold and stuffy to strangers. But at home, surrounded by friends, he showed another side of his character. He was charming, with a keen sense of humor. His pale face took on a rosy glow as he watched his guests roar with laughter at his stories.

Although a quiet, scholarly man, President James Madison led the nation during its second war with Great Britain.

Madison hoped for peace, although cries for war were growing louder. The loudest cries came not from the great shipping centers, but from the South and western frontier areas. The New England states and New York were willing to put up with a lot to prevent war. Having their ships searched and cargoes seized were costly nuisances, but not as costly as war, which would destroy the country's overseas trade altogether. As for impressment, there were always lots of young men eager to seek their fortunes at sea.

Although the South had few large seaports, and the West wasn't even near the ocean, they resented British high-handedness at sea. "Free trade and sailors' rights," they believed, were principles worth fighting for. So was the chance to end the Indian menace forever.

Southerners and frontiersmen lived in terror of the Indians, and the Indians' friends were the British. People in these areas had bitter memories of the Revolution, when British agents gave the tribes guns, ammunition and whiskey, then sent them to raid frontier settlements. British "hair buyers" paid bounties for American scalps, so much and so much for proof that a brave had killed a man, woman, or child.

Britain's defeat in the Revolution didn't end her friendship with the Indians; if anything, it drew them together more closely. Fort Malden, Canada, near where the Detroit River flows into Lake Erie, became the most important trading post in North America. Indians came there from hundreds of miles away to exchange furs for weapons and other things. British agents also gave them plenty of free advice — such as how nice it would be if they (the tribes) drove away the American settlers.

Beaver and muskrat furs brought top prices in Europe at this time. The richest source of these furs was the Indian lands of the Northwest Territory, the very area Americans began to flock into after the Revolution. Stretching from the Allegheny Mountains to the Mississippi River and from the Ohio River to the Great Lakes, eventually six states — Ohio, Illinois, Indiana, Michigan, Wisconsin, Minnesota — would be carved out of this huge territory. The British, however, urged the Indians to resist the Americans in order to keep the rich fur trade in their own hands.

But a group of Southern and Western congressmen called the War Hawks had other plans. Among them was John C. Calhoun of South Carolina, whose mother had been scalped by Cherokees. Felix Grundy of Tennessee had lost three brothers in Indian raids. The War Hawks' leader was the famous orator Henry Clay of Kentucky. Nicknamed "Harry of the West," Clay made no secret of his friends' plans. They would not rest until the United States broke the power of the Indian tribes and wiped out their base in Canada; indeed, they wanted to seize Canada and open its fertile lands to American settlers. Taking Canada, they thought, would be so easy. Clay boasted that a few Kentucky backwoodsmen would be able to do the job by themselves in a few weeks.

Frontiersmen were especially worried about Tecumseh, chief of the Shawnees. Tecumseh, whose name means "Panther-lying-in-wait," was born in 1768 near the present city of Dayton, Ohio. His earliest memories were of wars with land-hungry American settlers. His father was killed by settlers, and Tecumseh himself, although only a child, fought on the British side during the Revolution.

As he grew to manhood, Tecumseh became known everywhere on the frontier for his bravery and intelligence. There was something about him, something in the way he spoke and carried himself, that won other people's respect. Whites admired him and listened when he spoke. Tecumseh was never greedy or cruel; if he made a promise, nothing could make him go back on his word. At a time when it was Indian custom to torture war prisoners, he treated them with kindness and respect.

Like Henry Clay, the Shawnee chief was a great orator. Tecumseh had a powerful, booming voice that not only reached his listeners' ears, but into their hearts as well. His words, spoken with sincerity and deep feeling, called upon the Indians to be true to themselves, to give up the white man's ways. The Great Spirit, he said, hadn't made the red men to drink whiskey or wear cloth clothes, but to be a sober people who knew how to live by hunting and wore finely tanned buckskin.

Tecumseh reminded the Indians of how the Americans had taken millions of acres of their best land. If things continued as in the past, he warned that the tribes would lose everything, becoming beggars in their own country. He said: "Once there was not a white man in all this country. Then it all belonged to the red men, children of the same parents, placed on it by the Great Spirit, to keep it, to travel over it, to eat its fruits, and fill it with the same race. Once they were happy people, but now they are made hungry by the white people, who are never satisfied, who are always

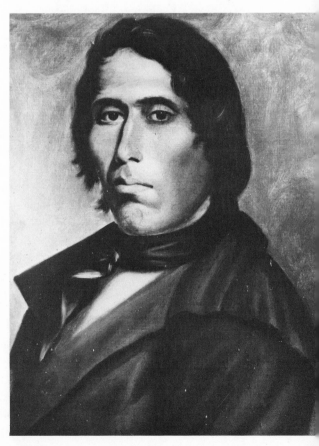

Tecumseh, the Shawnee Chief, dreamed of a united Indian nation to block the westward advance of the United States and preserve tribal lands.

encroaching on our land. They have driven us from the great salt water, forced us over the mountains, and would push us into the lakes. We are determined to go no further."

Tecumseh believed that the Indians could only save themselves if the tribes forgot their quarrels and joined together. He dreamed of a time when Indians would form a united nation stretching from the sweet water to the salt water, from the Great Lakes to the Gulf of Mexico. Such a nation would block the expansion of the United States, limiting it to a narrow strip along the Atlantic coast.

Tecumseh traveled thousands of miles each year preaching his message to the scattered tribes. His Indian nation actually began to take shape in a town he built along Tippecanoe Creek in northern Indiana. Shawnees, Wyandots, Ojibwas, Kickapoos, Delawares, and Ottawas came to live together as brothers in his town.

The settlers, knowing that Tecumseh would drive them out when he felt strong enough, decided to act before it was too late. Late in 1811, William Henry Harrison, Governor of the Indiana Territory, advanced on the Tippecanoe with a thousand-man army. He had chosen the perfect time to make his move, for Tecumseh was visiting the southern tribes and wasn't expected to return for months. Before leaving, the chief had warned the Prophet, his brother and second-in-command, not to fight until he returned. If the Americans came, the Prophet was to guard the town and promise them anything to avoid a battle.

The Prophet, however, was a hothead who disobeyed orders at the first opportunity. So sure was he of his magical powers that he promised the braves to make the Americans' guns harmless as grains of sand and their bullets soft as raindrops. He was mistaken. On November 7, 1811, he attacked Harrison's camp, only to find that his charms were no match for military discipline and firepower. The Americans shot the tribesmen down by the hundreds and burned their capital to the ground.

The Battle of Tippecanoe ended Tecumseh's dream of an Indian nation — for then. If that dream was ever to become a reality, he had to have a powerful ally. Early in

The Americans, under William Henry Harrison, defeated the braves of
Tecumseh's nation at the battle of Tippecanoe.

1812, the chief and hundreds of followers made their way to
Fort Malden, where the British welcomed them with open
arms. Tecumseh made camp outside the fort's wooden
stockade and bided his time, waiting for the big war he knew
was coming.

He didn't have to wait long. For early in June, 1812, the
War Hawks persuaded Congress to declare war on Great
Britain. On June 18, President Madison signed the declara-
tion of war and read his war message to both houses of
Congress. The United States, he said, had been forced to
fight another war because of Great Britain's impressment of
seamen, its Orders in Council, and its encouragement of
Indian uprisings on the frontier.

That night messengers leaped on their horses and galloped
out of Washington to spread the news. "Here's the stuff!"
Billy Phillips shouted as he tore through sleeping villages.
"WAR WITH ENGLAND! WAR!!"

2

Disaster on the Frontier

Americans were soon to learn that it is easier to declare war than to win victories. For war has a way of sending high hopes running head-on into reality. War is a dice game for the highest stakes, only more unpredictable and harder to control than some ivory cubes flung across a table.

Despite all the boasting, the American people and their armed forces were unprepared for war. The only thing united about the United States in 1812 was its name. People were not ready then to close ranks behind the war effort. Although Southerners and Westerners cheered the declaration of war, New Englanders greeted it with catcalls. "Mr. Madison's War," they called it as they lowered their flags to half-mast and draped their windows in black. A congressman from Plymouth, Massachusetts, who had voted for war was kicked through the streets by jeering townspeople. Throughout the war, hundreds of New Englanders traded with the enemy. The hooves of their cattle wore deep ruts in forest trails leading to the Canadian border, where they were sold to the British army for food.

The United States Army might do well against scattered Indian bands, but it had a lot to learn about fighting British regulars. "Regulars" belong to a national army, in which they serve full time for several years. Although Britain's army numbered three hundred thousand men, fewer than seven thousand could be spared from the war against Napoleon. Yet these were tough, disciplined veterans who knew their business.

The Americans also had about seven thousand regulars, mostly inexperienced recruits. These were supported by eight hundred thousand militiamen. Under the law, every able-bodied man had to give a few days a year to military training. This training usually meant parading on the village green, firing a few shots into the air, and settling down to a well-earned picnic in the shade. The militia could only be called out by their state's governor, and then only for a few weeks during emergencies. They could not be made to serve outside their home states.

Yet the United States Army's worst problem was not at the bottom, with its fighting men, but at the top, with their commanders. Its seven generals had served the nation well during the Revolution. Now they were in their sixties; proud and lazy, they hadn't led men in battle for thirty years, nor kept up with the science of war. Some, though, were good at overeating and emptying whiskey bottles. Henry Dearborn, the senior major general, was too fat to mount a horse and had to lead his troops from a buckboard.

"Granny" Dearborn, as the troops called him, drew up the master plan for the invasion of Canada. His plan was to send four invasion forces across the border at about the same time. One would move from Fort Detroit against Fort Malden, while two others set out from Sackett's Harbor and Fort Niagara in New York State. These would then link up with a fourth column advancing northward from Lake Champlain, and together they would capture Montreal, Canada's chief city.

Granny Dearborn's plan, though risky, promised to win the war quickly. Canada's border with the United States stretched for a thousand miles from Montreal on the Saint Lawrence River to Detroit at the western end of Lake Erie. Whoever controlled these waterways also controlled the land on either side of the border. For in 1812, the land was a roadless wilderness of virgin forests. By capturing key points along the waterways, the Americans hoped to cut enemy communications from East to West, easily winning the war.

The plan was set in motion by General William Hull, governor of the Michigan Territory. A hero of the Revolution, Hull, at sixty, was a red-faced, silver-haired gentleman who thought fighting should be left to younger men. But since President Madison insisted, he brushed aside his doubts and took command of the force aimed against Fort Malden.

Several weeks before the declaration of war, Hull gathered a two-thousand-man army of regulars and militiamen in Ohio and began to march north. It was rough going, and slow, since the army had to cross two hundred miles of unbroken wilderness. An advance unit of hundreds of axemen had to cut down trees, build bridges, and fill ravines to allow the main force to pass with its heavy equipment.

Even so, the soldiers suffered every step of the way. Each man wore a uniform consisting of a long blue coat over a white shirt and breeches. These uniforms were meant to look flashy on the parade ground, not for comfort on the march. There was no such thing as summer or winter gear; the soldiers wore the same uniform the year round. Although shirts and breeches were of linen, the coats were made of thick, scratchy wool cut to fit tight as a straightjacket. To make sure that the soldier stood straight, a high, stiff leather collar was placed under the chin. A black leather shako, or "tar bucket," served as a hat. Besides being heavy, the tar bucket had no brim to keep the sun out of the soldier's eyes.

Hull's men resembled human pack horses. Each soldier carried a fifty-pound pack, whose wide straps cut into his shoulders, raising red welts that burned when salty sweat ran over them. Then, as now, soldiers on campaign had little chance to wash. Instead, they rubbed the dirt off their necks and from between their toes, rolling it into little black balls. Lice nestled in the seams of their clothing, eager to bite the warm skin beneath. The soldiers stank, but since everyone stank alike, no one noticed.

Men slept at night from sheer exhaustion. They certainly weren't comfortable, for there were few tents or blankets and no waterproof groundcloths to protect from dampness. Each soldier simply lay down on the safest, dryest piece of ground he could find. If it rained, he slept soaked to the skin, or not at all. If the temperature dropped, he lay awake with chattering teeth. Yet no matter how tired or uncomfortable the troops were, the bugle always sounded an hour before sunup for the morning stand-to. Since dawn is a perfect time for surprise attacks, the soldiers always greeted the new day in battle formation. Only when they could see clearly for a half-mile in every direction did the bugle sound breakfast call.

The soldier's main weapon was the muzzle-loading musket. This weapon weighed eleven pounds, was just under five feet long, and shot a one-ounce lead ball that could mangle a person horribly. Loading and firing a musket was no easy task. To load, the soldier took a cartridge from a leather-covered box attached to his belt. This cartridge was a paper tube containing a bullet and gunpowder. The soldier, standing, bit the cartridge open and sprinkled some powder onto the pan above the trigger; beneath the pan was a narrow opening leading to the inside of the gun barrel. He then poured the rest of the cartridge down the muzzle, crumpled the paper into a wad, and packed everything tightly with a ramrod. To fire, he put the musket on his shoulder, drew back the hammer, and pulled the trigger. The falling hammer struck a flint, which sent a spark into the powder-filled pan, exploding the main charge in the barrel.

The musket was an unreliable weapon. In damp weather, let alone in a rainstorm, the powder wouldn't explode. Yet even on the best days a soldier could only fire two or three shots a minute, and these nearly always missed. The musket was so inaccurate that one officer calculated that it took four hundred fifty shots to hit one enemy. Even if a bullet did strike, it lost so much force traveling through the air that it couldn't kill beyond a hundred yards. The deadliest part of the musket wasn't its bullets, but the twenty-one-inch bayonet attached to its muzzle. Most battles were won not by gunfire, but by a massed bayonet charge.

Soldiers were perhaps more frightened by their own army surgeons than of being killed outright by the enemy. Treatment of gunshot wounds was very simple and very painful. If the wound wasn't serious, the surgeon washed and cauterized it; that is, he closed it with a red-hot knife blade. Someone seriously wounded in the arm or leg faced the ordeal of amputation. Since there were no painkillers in 1812, a wounded soldier was gotten drunk or made to "bite the bullet." As he held a bullet between his teeth, strong men held him down while a surgeon worked as quickly as possible. Many died of pain during the operation. Others died afterward, from infection, because no one had yet discovered that germs cause disease and that surgical instruments must be sterilized. Deep wounds in the stomach or chest couldn't be treated at all; the best the surgeon could do was to make the patient as comfortable as possible and hope he wouldn't suffer too much before dying.

Hull's soldiers must have had these dangers in mind as they approached Fort Detroit early in July. After resting his troops for a few days, the general led them across the Detroit River. Their destination: Fort Malden.

At first the invasion seemed more like a victorious parade than real war. Except for some Indian snipers, there was no opposition; indeed, French-Canadians, who hated the British, offered to join the Americans.

The road to Fort Malden lay open. The fort itself was weak, defended by a handful of regulars and militiamen. Built of wood, it was meant to withstand Indian attacks, not cannon. Hull's artillery could easily have battered the wooden stockade to splinters and set fire to the shingle-roofed buildings. Yet William Hull was losing his nerve with every passing mile.

The general knew that invading Canada was taking a chance, one that might cost him everything. For as he advanced, his supply line grew longer. A shrewd enemy could snap that line any moment, leaving his army stranded. To the east, on his right, the supply line passed along the shore of Lake Erie, which the British controlled; they had six small gunboats, the Americans none. To the west, on his left, Indians loyal to Tecumseh prowled the forests. Thus, instead of trying to capture Fort Malden quickly, Hull moved slowly, cautiously. *Too* slowly; *too* cautiously.

On July 28, Hull received news that a British-Indian raiding party had captured Fort Mackinac at the northern entrance to Lake Huron. That news threw him into a panic. His imagination ran wild, filled with nightmares of Indians cutting his supply line and massacring defenseless settlers in the Michigan Territory. He became so worried that he could think of nothing better to do than order the army to pack up and retreat to the safety of Fort Detroit.

Now came the enemy's turn to advance. Hull's invasion had taken the British by surprise. But when they realized after a few days that he was moving at a snail's pace, they began to rush reinforcements to Fort Malden. Those troops were commanded by General Isaac Brock, a fine soldier and one of Canada's greatest heroes. At forty-three, the blond, blue-eyed general stood six feet three inches tall, a man-mountain of muscle and bone. Brock could wrestle, box, and swim like a champion. He feared no man. When, as a young officer, a bully challenged him to a duel, he accepted, insisting only that they fight toe-to-toe with pistols. The bully swallowed hard, ran, and was never seen again.

During his first night at Fort Malden, Brock heard a knock at his office door. A colonel entered the room, followed by a group of Indians. "This, sir," he said, pointing to a tall brave, "is Tecumseh, who desires to meet you." Brock saw a man who, though shorter than himself, was as solidly built. He stood erect, shoulders back, chest out. Here was a proud, strong-willed man who knew what he wanted. He wore a buckskin jacket and leggings; on his feet were moccasins decorated with brightly colored porcupine quills. A single eagle feather flashed in his black hair. Three silver coins dangled from his nose.

They liked each other, it seems, even before the colonel translated their greetings. Tecumseh turned to his aides and gave Brock the highest compliment a Shawnee could give another: *"This is a man!"* The braves nodded in agreement, muttering *"Ho! Ho!"*

The greeting completed, Tecumseh knelt on the ground and unrolled a sheet of elm bark. His scalping knife gleamed in the candlelight as he scratched a map of the Detroit area on the bark, complete with streams and forest paths. The red and white chiefs understood each other immediately, without words. Neither wanted to waste time before dealing with the Americans.

Detroit in 1812 was a thriving settlement of eight hundred residents. Both the town and its protecting fort were surrounded by a high stockade of logs sharpened to points at the top. Hundreds of loopholes had been bored into the stockade to allow soldiers to fire their muskets without exposing themselves. Heavy cannon captured from the British during the Revolution were zeroed in on the approaches to the fort. Some cannon were double-loaded with eight- or twelve-pound balls of solid iron. Others were loaded with canister shot, thin-skinned metal cans or canvas bags filled with hundreds of musket balls. No soldier, however brave, could look forward to attacking in the face of these giant shotguns.

Brock set out on August 15 with three hundred regulars, four hundred Canadian militiamen, and six hundred Indians; that is, thirteen hundred attackers against more than two thousand defenders. Outnumbered though he was, the Englishman knew he had a powerful ally inside the fort. That ally was William Hull, or, rather, Hull's own fears.

Brock did whatever he could to keep those fears alive. He dressed his militiamen in red coats to make the Americans think they were up against a large body of regulars. He also sent Hull a letter warning that, unless the fort surrendered immediately, he might not be able to prevent an Indian massacre if it had to be taken by force. Brock even allowed a British messenger to be captured with a false letter saying that he already had five thousand Indian warriors and didn't need reinforcements from Mackinac.

As the sun set, Tecumseh's braves silently waded into the Detroit River and crossed to the American shore. The Indians looked ferocious, like creatures from another world. Naked except for moccasins and a loincloth, they were armed with muskets, tomahawks, spears, bows and arrows, scalping knives, and stone-headed war clubs. Each brave's hair was plastered stiff with bear grease and resembled bristling porcupine quills. His body was painted in weird designs and color combinations: all white or black; half black and half white or half red. These patterns were supposed to give the brave magical protection and make him blend into the forest's dim light and moving shadows.

Quietly, without snapping a twig, Tecumseh's men encircled Detroit, cutting it off from the outside world. All night the guards on the stockade heard more wild turkey calls and coyote cries than ever before. The Indians were "talking" to one another in a language only they understood.

In the morning, August 16, Brock led his main force across the river. Tecumseh's warriors were whooping and hollering with excitement as the Redcoats lined up for a head-on assault. It is untrue that the bright color of the British regular's coat made him an easy target. Muskets were so inaccurate, and battles fought at such close range, that the color of one's coat had nothing to do with whether he was hit or not. In fact, the red coat was *supposed* to make its wearer highly visible. Bright red allowed friendly troops to identify one another through the "fog of battle," the thick clouds of smoke given off by the old-style gunpowder. Unlike the blue-coated Americans and French, the "Lobsterbacks" seldom shot at one another by mistake. One other advantage: the red coat hid blood, preventing others from getting jittery if a neighbor was badly wounded and became covered with blood.

Brock's Redcoats waited for their artillery to soften up the fort before charging. Their cannon banged away for several minutes, doing little damage until a ball landed in the midst of a group of American officers, killing three. Seeing this, Hull became paralyzed with fear. Unable to decide what to do next, he sat in his office stuffing his mouth with chewing tobacco without noticing the yellow-brown saliva dribbling down his beard and over his shirt.

Outside, Detroit's defenders only needed their general's order to open fire. Instead, they saw their flag flutter down the flagpole and a white sheet run up in its place. General Hull, fearing that the people in the fort, including his daughter and grandchildren, would be massacred, had sur-

General William Hull (right) hands his sword to General Isaac Brock during the surrender of Fort Detroit.

rendered without firing a shot. This was the only time a city of the United States has ever surrendered to a foreign enemy.

Hull's men were shocked. Many couldn't believe the surrender was real, but when they learned the truth they broke their swords and smashed their muskets in anger. They felt dishonored, for besides outnumbering the enemy, they had plenty of food and ammunition for a siege.

Brock was also shocked, unable to believe that he had won the whole Michigan Territory without losing a man. Later that day he led his officers into the fort, where they knelt and kissed the cannon captured from their countrymen so long ago.

The American prisoners were treated well. The militiamen were sent home after promising not to fight again during the war. The regulars, including their general, were sent to a prison camp in Canada. Hull was later sent home in exchange for British captives. He was tried at court-martial and sentenced to be shot for cowardice. President Madison, however, pardoned him because of his services during the Revolution.

Tecumseh made sure that American civilians weren't mistreated. One day, as he spoke to his braves, he felt a tugging on his deerskin jacket. Looking down, he saw a small white girl of about eight or nine. He smiled at her and continued speaking. More tugging. "Come to our house," she said. "Some bad Indians are at our house."

Tecumseh ran in the direction she pointed until he came to a log cabin, the home of Mrs. Ruland and her children. Just then the front door swung open and he saw three Indians begin to drag out a trunk. He was furious. They had disobeyed his orders against looting and must pay with their lives. "Dogs!" he shouted, "I am Tecumseh!" One blow of his tomahawk dropped the leader and sent the others dashing into the forest. Behind them, inside the house, he glimpsed some Redcoats. "You, you are worse than dogs!" he bellowed at the top of his voice. The soldiers backed out the door, apologizing to Mrs. Ruland as they went. Later, when an officer promised to put a guard at the house, she refused.

"No," she said, pointing to the Shawnee chief. "So long as that man is around, we feel safe." Unfortunately, Tecumseh couldn't be everywhere.

*   *   *

A dreadful massacre took place on August 15, 1812, the day before Hull's surrender. While still in Canada, the general sent orders for the garrison at Fort Dearborn to retreat to Fort Wayne, a larger post and safer from Indian attack. Fort Dearborn, named in honor of General "Granny" Dearborn, stood on the bank of the Chicago River, on the site of the future city of Chicago, Illinois. Except for Lake Michigan nearby, the fort was surrounded by villages of the Potawatami, allies of Tecumseh who saw the whites as invaders to be exterminated.

Fort Dearborn's commander was Captain Nathan Heald. A stubborn man, Heald ignored the warnings of Catfish, a friendly Potawatami, that it would be suicidal to leave the fort. Nor did he listen when his own men said they'd rather take their chances in the fort than risk being caught in the open. But Captain Heald couldn't think beyond his orders. All he knew was that the general wanted something done, and he'd do it or die trying.

At nine o'clock in the morning, about a hundred soldiers and civilians left Fort Dearborn. The soldiers knew they were heading for trouble, and their band struck up a funeral march for the occasion. The column had gone only a mile, to some sand dunes along the shore of Lake Michigan, when five hundred Potawatamis streamed out of the woods. The braves were terrifying in their war paint and feathers. The soldiers gripped their muskets, while inside the wagons mothers hugged their whimpering children.

A war whoop split the air as the Indians opened fire. With people falling all around, the wagon drivers whipped their horses into a gallop. Minutes seemed like hours, until the column reached a clump of trees, where the soldiers prepared for a last stand.

Captain Heald, however, was able to call a truce and work out a surrender that allowed the survivors to become prisoners of war until the government paid for their release. Yet there was a catch, for only the unwounded were allowed to surrender. The Indians went over the battlefield killing and scalping the wounded. Heald's stubbornness had cost the lives of fifty-four people, including twelve children killed in a single wagon. Fort Dearborn was burned to the ground.

News of the Dearborn Massacre sent a shiver of fear throughout the frontier. Pioneers by the hundreds abandoned their farms and crowded into the forts for safety. Those who couldn't be warned in time were killed in their sleep or cut down in their fields. The lucky ones, some of them, were warned when a knock came at their cabin door. Opening it, they saw a man whose face was covered with a wild, shaggy beard. A tin pot served as his hat; his shirt was an old coffee sack with holes cut for his head and arms. As the farmer blinked his eyes in amazement, the stranger chanted:

> I sow while others reap.
> Be sure my warning keep.
> Indians will come by break of day.
> Indians hunting scalps, I say.

With that, Johnny Appleseed walked off into the forest gloom. His real name was John Chapman, and for years he roamed the frontier giving apple seeds to the farmers and planting them on his own. The Indians, who believed he had been sent by the Great Spirit, left him alone even in wartime. They let him come and go as he pleased, and his warnings about their attacks always proved correct.

*   *   *

General Brock, meanwhile, had hurried back to Fort George, his headquarters on the Niagara River a few miles below the famous Falls. Brock wanted to strengthen his defenses along the New York-Canada border, where he believed the Americans would attack next.

Brock's hunch turned out to be right. Major General Stephen van Rensselaer had gathered an army across the Niagara River from Queenston, Ontario. Despite his careful planning, the operation got off to a bad start when an officer rowed to the Canadian side in a boat with all the expedition's oars and left it there. After replacing the oars, van Rensselaer tried again on the night of October 13, 1812. Since there weren't enough boats to carry the whole four-thousand-man army at once, they had to shuttle back and forth in the darkness many times.

Fewer than half the troops had landed when a Redcoat sentry saw them and gave the alarm. Tongues of flame cut the darkness as a handful of British troops and Canadian militiamen, many startled out of a deep sleep, rushed to meet the enemy. The pop, pop, popping of musketry was soon drowned by the roar of artillery as the British gunners opened fire on the boats in midstream.

The sound of gunfire carried to Fort George seven miles away, awakening Brock. The general sent messengers galloping to every outpost in the area, then, mounting his horse, led his own troops toward Queenston. He arrived to find the Americans dug in on the high ground above the town. Without hesitating, he led a charge up the steep hill. Dressed in a scarlet coat with gold braiding, the big man on the white horse was a target for every American; infantrymen made a special point of concentrating their fire on mounted officers. Brock was already wounded in the wrist when he felt a sharp, hot sting in his chest. He tumbled to the ground, living only long enough to warn his officers not to tell their men what had happened. The brave general feared that his troops might lose courage if they learned of his death.

Gradually, as the day wore on, British reinforcements began to turn the tide of battle. Van Rensselaer's only hope now was to bring the rest of his army across the river as soon as possible. It didn't take him long to discover, however, that he no longer commanded an army. The troops on the New York side were mostly militiamen who had lost their taste for fighting. The sight of returning wounded, many of them horribily mangled, frightened them to the point where nothing could make them go into action. When van Rensselaer begged them to help their friends across the river, they either turned away or refused, claiming their right as militiamen not to fight outside their home state. Thus, by sundown nearly every one of the nine hundred men who had landed in Canada was dead or a prisoner.

The other parts of Granny Dearborn's invasion plan collapsed soon afterward. Dearborn himself led six thousand regulars and militiamen from Plattsburg, New York, on Lake Champlain, to the border, where half that number of enemy troops were waiting. Once again American militia refused to fight. The season's first snows were falling when Dearborn marched his army, weary but happy, to cosy winter quarters at Plattsburg. The invasion from Sackett's Harbor on Lake Ontario never even got started.

Englishmen read the news from North America and smiled. Except for the fact that people were dying, the war on land seemed a joke. Nothing the enemy did went right; nothing their own generals did went wrong. The Americans of 1812, they said, were soft compared to those who had won the Revolution. These Yankees would be a soft nut to crack. Just wait till 1813.

The character of Uncle Sam was born at this time, not as a symbol of national pride, but of the federal government's failures. "Uncle Sam" was the nickname of Samuel Wilson, an army meat inspector from Troy, New York. Since Wilson stamped a large U.S. (for United States) on the barrels of salted meat he approved, local people, who knew him as a rascal, began to joke about U.S.-marked equipment from brass buttons to bullets. If it belonged to Uncle Sam (the federal government), it couldn't be any good.

*   *   *

The New Year was a gloomy time for the American people. The task now wasn't to conquer Canada, but to recapture the Michigan Territory. A new commander was needed in the West, a younger man who would fight. That man was William Henry Harrison, the hero of Tippecanoe. Early in the New Year, the thirty-nine-year-old governor of Indiana Territory became a major general in the regular army. What others had wrecked, he would have to rebuild.

Harrison's plan was to march from Ohio to the Maumee

River south of Fort Detroit, where he'd build a fort and prepare for the spring campaign. His army of about six thousand men would advance in three columns so that the enemy wouldn't learn of his intentions until the last moment, when it would be too late to do anything about them.

One column was made up of Kentucky volunteers under Brigadier General James Winchester. No sooner had the column reached the frozen Maumee when it received a call for help from Frenchtown, a tiny settlement on the River Raisin in Michigan. British troops and Indians were in the area and the settlers were scared for their lives.

Winchester marched to the rescue at top speed. It was bitterly cold. The wind howled at ten degrees below zero, knocking the heavily loaded troops down and sending them skidding across the ice-covered Maumee. The general was so glad to reach shelter in Frenchtown that he forgot to send out patrols to check the enemy's whereabouts.

That mistake cost the Americans dearly. Their camp-fires were beacons carefully watched from the surrounding forest darkness. As the exhausted soldiers slept, two thousand Redcoats and braves prepared to attack. Their commander was Major General Henry A. Proctor, the new British chief in the West. Unlike Brock, whose place he took, Proctor's courage came, not from inner strength, but from having lots of armed men to do his work. He was a weakling who, we'll see, blamed others for his mistakes. Tecumseh hated him and called him a coward to his face. But on this morning of January 23, 1813, the Shawnee chief was on another of his journeys to rouse the Southern tribes, allowing the weakling to command all by himself.

A heavy snow had begun to fall when, at four o'clock in the morning, the ground shook as artillery fire tore into Frenchtown and the sleeping camp. Through the swirling snow and gunsmoke came the Redcoats with fixed bayonets. Tomahawk-waving braves poured into the American position from behind.

The surprise was total. After a brief, brutal fight, Winchester had to surrender his whole force of eight hundred fifty men or face annihilation. Proctor promised as part of

General William Henry Harrison in a portrait made later in life.

the surrender terms that the Americans would be treated according to the laws of war. He gave his word of honor as a soldier that his captives would receive food, shelter, medical attention, and protection. Unfortunately, his word meant nothing.

No sooner had the Americans put down their muskets when the Indians stripped them of their warm coats and anything else that attracted their attention. On the march back to Fort Malden the prisoners were forced to take over from the horses and pull the heavy sleds through the snow drifts.

These were the lucky ones; they lived. Their wounded friends, about sixty-four officers and men, were left behind in Frenchtown. Proctor had promised that they would be protected and that sleds would be sent to take them to Fort Malden in a couple of days. But as the column began to move, a British officer told an American, "The Indians are excellent doctors."

The wounded learned what he meant that night. Frenchtown had thirty houses, among which the wounded were distributed. Outside, they could hear the Indians whooping and the smashing of glass and furniture. The braves were looting the houses, breaking everything they couldn't use. Somehow they found kegs of "rotgut," the coarse, powerful whiskey made by frontiersmen. Drunkenness made them crazy, so crazy that they killed the wounded as they lay helpless in bed. The bodies were scalped and the trophies sent to Proctor at Fort Malden.

A young Kentuckian named A. G. Austen was a prisoner at the fort when the scalps arrived. He wrote his mother next day:

> Never, dear mother, if I should live a thousand years, can I forget the frightful sight of this morning, when handsomely painted Indians came into the fort, some of them carrying half a dozen scalps of my countrymen fastened upon sticks, and yet covered with blood, and were congratulated by [General] Proctor for their *bravery*. I heard a British officer . . . tell another officer . . . that Proctor was a disgrace to the British army . . . [and] a blot upon the British character.

Kentucky went into mourning for its massacred sons. Its sadness though, was mingled with a call for vengeance. The cry "Remember the Raisin" echoed across the land and would some day be carried deep into Canada.

General Harrison also remembered the Raisin. During the weeks following the massacre, he worked his men double-time to finish their fort on the Maumee, which he named Fort Meigs in honor of the governor of Ohio. He had enough of fighting for a while and was determined to sit tight until

"Remember the Raisin!" frontiersmen cried when they heard of the Indian massacre of prisoners at Frenchtown on the River Raisin in 1813.

the spring thaw allowed reinforcements to come from Kentucky; then he'd go on the offensive.

The Kentuckians were on their way when, in May, 1813, Proctor decided to attack first. As usual, the British advanced behind a screen of Indians, only now Tecumseh was with the army, having recently returned from the South. Tecumseh had wanted to settle scores with Harrison ever since the Battle of Tippecanoe. The moment his braves surrounded Fort Meigs, he sent a letter challenging the American general to come out and fight:

> I have with me eight hundred braves. You have an equal number in your hiding place. Come out with them and give me a battle. You talked like a brave man when we met at Vincennes (the capital of Indiana Territory), and I respected you, but now you hide behind logs and in the earth, like a groundhog. Give me your answer.
>
> — Tecumseh

Harrison didn't reply. Of course he'd fight Tecumseh, but he alone would choose the time and place of their showdown.

Harrison worried more about his reinforcements than about the troops bottled up in the fort; at least they had a stockade and cannon between them and the enemy. The Kentuckians, however, were traveling through strange country patrolled by Indian scouts.

His fears proved justified a few days later. When Tecumseh learned that the Kentuckians were nearby, he set an ambush on the north bank of the Maumee, across from Fort Meigs. They didn't have a chance. Redcoats and Indians hit them so suddenly and so hard that they collapsed as a military force. "Every man for himself!" someone shouted as the whole unit broke and ran. Four hundred eighty Kentuckians were killed, one hundred fifty captured. Having won his victory, Tecumseh started back to Fort Meigs. The prisoners were marched by a small British guard detail to their main camp further downstream.

The prisoners' sense of doom increased every step of the way. Indians pressed alongside the column and began to take their clothing, leaving them practically naked. The wounded were jabbed with spears to make them move faster. Arriving at the camp, the Kentuckians found two lines of braves awaiting them. They'd have to run the gauntlet, passing between the lines as the Indians lashed out with war clubs, tomahawks, and scalping knives.

The noise was deafening as war whoops mingled with the dull thud of weapons striking flesh and the screams of the injured. The lucky ones reached the end of the gauntlet with cuts and broken bones. The unlucky ones were killed if they stumbled and their bodies tossed into a ditch to be scalped later.

The terror continued inside the camp itself. Prisoners were huddled together, not knowing what to expect, when suddenly a huge brave waded into the crowd. He was naked and painted black from head to toe. Calmly, he shot a prisoner, reloaded his gun, and shot another. A massacre was underway, but a British officer standing nearby could only say, smilingly, "*Oh, nichee wah!*" — "Oh, brother, quit it!"

Just when it seemed that the tragedy of the River Raisin would be repeated, a commotion was heard at the edge of the crowd. Tecumseh had arrived. Another British officer, a man of conscience, had sent a scout galloping after the Shawnee chief with a message to return while there was still time.

Tecumseh rode like an avenging storm. A British colonel who saw him later recalled, "His eyes shot fire. He was terrible." As he plunged through the mob he saw a brave standing over a prisoner with an uplifted tomahawk. Drawing a sword, he rode straight at the brave. THWACK! A blow over the head stretched the brave senseless on the ground.

Tecumseh saves American prisoners after ambushing them near Fort Meigs.

The mob had tasted blood and Tecumseh's own life was now in danger. He didn't care. Leaping from the horse, he stepped between the Indians and the Kentuckians. He grabbed a warrior by the throat and flung him to the ground. Another he slapped in the face with all his might, insulting him in front of everyone. "Are there no men here?" Tecumseh roared. The mob backed off, cowed by one fearless man of honor.

When they were gone, and he could calm down, a look of sadness came over the chief's face. Of course, he didn't cry; braves were taught from birth not to show emotion through tears. Yet that sad expression was the same as tears for Tecumseh.

"My poor Indians! My poor Indians!" he moaned. For Tecumseh, too, was afraid — afraid for his people and what the future held for them. How could his dream of an independent Indian nation come true if its citizens couldn't control their anger? How could they gain other peoples' respect if they acted like a bloodthirsty mob? And without self-control and respect, the American Indian was doomed.

Tecumseh's sadness again turned to anger when he thought of Proctor. He stormed across the camp and found the redcoated general standing with his staff. He came right to the point. Proctor should have protected the prisoners. He hadn't. Why?

The Englishman drew himself up to his full height and, pursing his lips, replied, "Your Indians cannot be controlled; they cannot be commanded."

Tecumseh had just proven the opposite. But then, Tecumseh was a brave man. The chief glared at the general, then, pausing a moment, spat out the worst insult a brave could give. He called Proctor a *squaw*, a woman. "Begone!" he cried, shaking with rage. "You are unfit to command. Go put on petticoats. I conquer to save, and you to murder." Proctor turned away without noticing that his officers had bent their heads and were staring down at their boots.

A few days later, May 5, 1813, the British gave up the siege of Fort Meigs and returned to Fort Malden. They returned for a second try in July, but retreated when it became clear that the Americans were dug in too well. General Harrison breathed a sigh of relief and set about rebuilding his army — again. The British had not heard the last of William Henry Harrison.

*   *   *

Thus, after exactly a year's fighting, the United States had nothing to show for its efforts on land except massacred citizens, lost territory, an army in disgrace, and an emptying treasury. Yet the War of 1812 had only begun. The worst, and the best, still lay ahead.

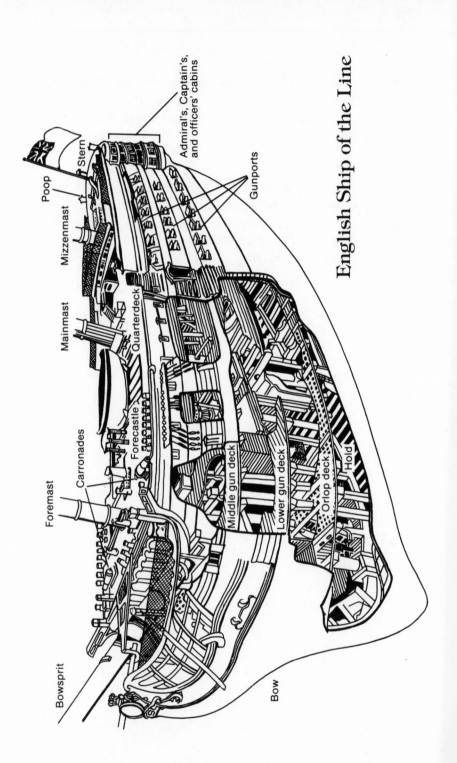

English Ship of the Line

Bowsprit

Foremast

Carronades

Forecastle

Quarterdeck

Mainmast

Mizzenmast

Poop

Stern

Admiral's, Captain's,
and officers' cabins

Gunports

Middle gun deck

Lower gun deck

Orlop deck

Hold

Bow

3
Fighting Frigates

The one thing you can count on in war is that things seldom turn out as planned. War is full of surprises, and often a nation does poorly where it expects to succeed, but succeeds where it expects to fail. So it was in the War of 1812. Instead of being a "frontiersman's frolic," as Jefferson predicted about the invasion of Canada, it became a disaster. But on the high seas, where most people expected the United States to be defeated so easily, her navy chalked up brilliant victories. In order to understand how these victories were won, we must first understand the ABC's of fighting in the Age of Sail.

* * *

Navies in the early 1800s depended upon three main types of warships. The first type was the ship of the line or line-of-battleship, later known simply as the battleship. Weighing in at over twenty-five-hundred tons, ships of the line carried from sixty-four to one hundred twenty cannon arranged on two or three levels, or gun decks. Slow and clumsy, these

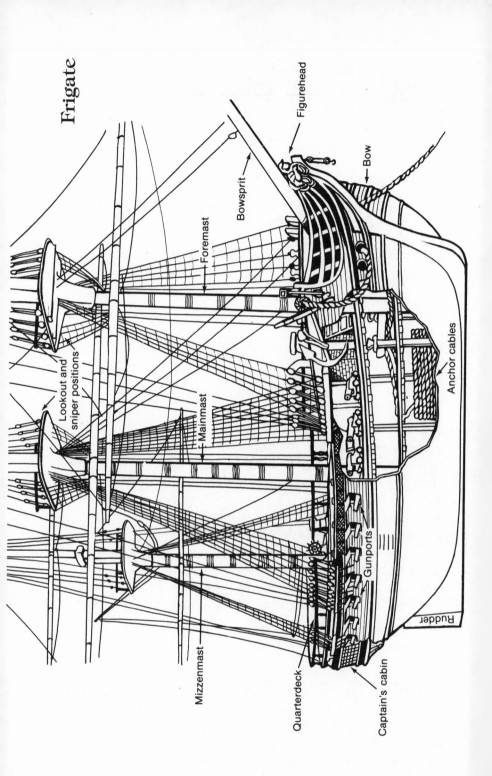

Frigate

- Figurehead
- Bow
- Bowsprit
- Foremast
- Lookout and sniper positions
- Mainmast
- Anchor cables
- Mizzenmast
- Quarterdeck
- Gunports
- Captain's cabin
- Rudder

floating fortresses were unstoppable except by vessels of their own class.

Next in importance was the frigate. A thousand tons lighter than their big sisters, frigates were called "the cavalry of the sea" because of their swiftness and ease of handling. Frigates carried between thirty-two and forty-four cannon set up on a single gun deck. Although they never fought ships of the line, these sleek, tall-masted beauties were excellent at scouting and hunting enemy merchant ships.

Sloops of war, the last warship type, mounted sixteen to twenty-four light cannon. Depending upon the number of masts and arrangement of the sails, sloops might be known as brigs, brigantines, and schooners. These lightweights were ideal for patrolling shallow offshore waters and blockading harbor entrances.

A warship's crew ranged from nine hundred men in the largest vessels to sixty in the smallest. Whether British or American, sailors were called "jack-tars," because they were men (jacks) who always seemed to smell of the tar used in waterproofing their vessels.

Unlike soldiers ashore, jack-tars had to dress comfortably in order to handle the ship. Sailors in both navies wore blue jackets and white trousers. Since they liked to braid their hair into a pigtail, which they greased with hog fat, a black scarf was worn to protect the jacket. Most sailors went barefooted, so that the soles of their feet became tough as old leather. Going barefoot gave a better grip on the slippery decks and made it easier to climb the masts when the sails had to be taken down and furled. Officers, however, were gentlemen who wore high boots, tight breeches, and blue coats loaded with gold braid and brass buttons.

Ships and seamen existed for one purpose: to provide a solid, steady platform for the big guns. Naval guns were larger than army artillery, which had to be dragged to the battlefield by horses or men. Warship guns were either of a long or short type. Long guns had long barrels (nine to ten feet) for sending shot long distances. Such weapons usually fired iron balls (shot) weighing twelve, eighteen, or twenty-four pounds apiece. A twenty-four-pounder long gun could put a hole in a vessel a mile and a half away. But since these balls traveled at very high speed, the holes they made were round, clean, and easy to plug with sheets of lead kept for the purpose.

Holes made by the carronade, or short gun, were different. The carronade took its name from its inventor, the Carron Iron Company of Scotland. Just five feet long, the carronade could throw a ball only half a mile. But these balls weighted forty-two or sixty-eight pounds. Since they traveled slowly, they made huge, jagged holes and sent more splinters through the air; splinters usually killed and wounded more men than solid shot. Wooden kegs filled with musket balls were often fired along with the cannonballs. No wonder sailors dreaded the carronade, calling it the "smasher" and "devil gun."

Each gun was manned by a crew of five to nine men, depending upon its size. Gunners' whole lives at sea were

Carronade

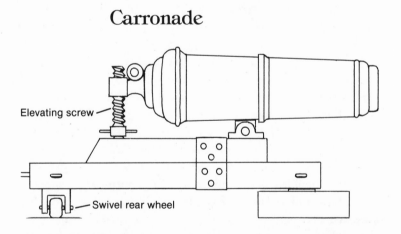

The short-barreled carronade, or smasher, cannon was a deadly close-range weapon that fired a very heavy ball. It was mounted on a special gun carriage, whose rear wheel allowed it to be swiveled for easier aiming. The threaded elevating screw at the rear was used to raise and lower the barrel more easily than a normal long-range gun.

spent in caring for their iron monsters. Day in and day out they cleaned and polished their guns, making sure they'd be in working order when needed. Gunners always stayed near their weapons; they even slept with them, or, rather, over them in hammocks suspended from the ceiling of the gun deck.

Getting a gun into action was difficult, dangerous work. Each step had to be taken in order, otherwise the weapon would jam or, worse, explode and kill its crew. Loading began with the gunpowder. Since gunpowder was dangerous, warships had a special storeroom, the magazine, built on the lowest deck, right above the water. Here thousands of cannon cartridges, each containing five to eight pounds of gunpowder, stood in racks along the walls. In case of fire, the magazine master turned a knob to open overhead water tanks, flooding the room in seconds. He had only seconds, for there had been accidents in which ships-of-the-line were blown sky-high, leaving no survivors.

During battle the cartridges were hoisted up to the "powder monkeys" waiting on the gun decks. Each gun crew had a powder monkey, a boy of eleven or twelve, whose job was to bring fresh cartridges as needed. The youngster placed the cartridge under his shirt and ran to the gun, hoping that flying cinders wouldn't set it off.

The cartridge was put down the cannon's muzzle with a long wooden-handled spoon with its sides turned up. A wad of shredded rope was then packed tightly over it with a rammer, a great wooden knob at the end of a pole. Lastly, the shot was rolled down and rammed tight with another rope wad on top of it. To fire, the gun captain poked a long, thin corkscrew down the touchhole to cut into the cartridge below. He then poured fine-grained gunpowder from a powder horn into the touchhole. When the target came into view, he set off the charge with a slow match, a smoldering rope soaked in lime to make it burn for hours. After each shot, the soot and burning pieces of wadding that stuck to the inside of the barrel had to be cleaned out with a "sponge," that is, a damp mop made of sheepskin wool. Terrible accidents happened when a fresh cartridge was rammed into an improperly cleaned barrel. A well-trained crew needed only a minute to load, fire, and reload.

Naval guns fired different kinds of shot for different purposes. As with land artillery, large iron balls and canister were used to punch holes in targets and mow down men. In addition, chain shot, or two balls attached to an iron chain, whirled through the air like a buzzsaw, bringing down the enemy's masts. Spider shot cut rope and slashed sails to ribbons with its two-foot-long blades fastened to an iron ring; bar shot, a smaller version of the weightlifter's dumbbells, served the same purpose. Grape shot was a collection of two-pound balls tied in a canvas bag to resemble a bunch of grapes; it knocked down masts, shredded ropes, and sliced

Typical Muzzle-Loading Cannon and Equipment

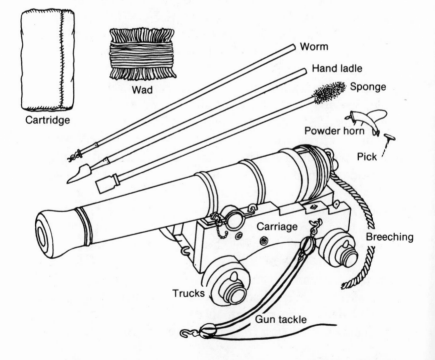

Cartridge

Wad

Worm

Hand ladle

Sponge

Powder horn

Pick

Carriage

Breeching

Trucks

Gun tackle

Types of Shot

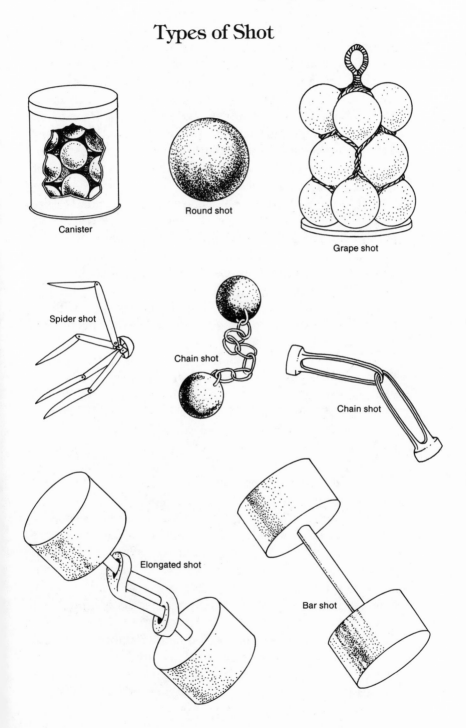

Canister

Round shot

Grape shot

Spider shot

Chain shot

Chain shot

Elongated shot

Bar shot

through chains. Hot shot was prepared in a furnace kept on the gun deck. When the ball became red-hot, it was lifted with tongs and placed in the gun barrel on top of a wet pad. Passing through the hull of an enemy vessel, hot shot immediately started internal fires, endangering the magazine.

Handling a man-of-war in battle was work for experts. Officers and sailing masters, who actually steered the vessels, were like dance instructors. Battle tactics in the Age of Sail were like a formal dance—a ballet danced to the tune of roaring cannon and men's screams.

Battles always began the same way. If whole fleets were involved, the ships of the line arranged themselves in two parallel lines of battle. Moving ahead as quickly as possible, they fired their broadsides as the distance between the lines closed. The object was for one line to get ahead of the other, passing it at right angles. This "crossing the T" let the full broadside of the faster fleet blast the enemy line without the enemy being able to bring more than a few guns to bear at a time.

The same principle applied when frigates, too light to fight in the line, met one-on-one. Each captain tried to set his vessel at right angles to the enemy's bow or stern and "rake" him; that is, send broadsides down his full length. Nearly every ball hit something during a raking, turning the enemy's deck into a bloody shambles. Once a broadside had been fired, the sailing master tried to turn the ship around to fire a broadside from the opposite decks, giving the first gun crews time to reload their weapons.

A wooden warship was almost impossible to sink by gunnery alone. Unless fire broke out, or some lucky shot struck below the waterline, it could stay afloat even after a terrific pounding. The big gun's real job was to soften up the enemy for the final blow by destroying his masts, sails, and steering gear. The battle only reached its height as the ships were deliberately run into each other. Now the sea fight became an old-fashioned land battle fought by soldiers.

Marines were the "soldiers of the sea." Every man-of-war carried up to one hundred marines, whose normal duty was as ship's police and guards. Marines with muskets and fixed bayonets stood outside the captain's cabin, the magazine, and the room where the rum barrels were stored. As policemen, marines were discouraged from becoming friendly with the crew. Marines formed a separate little community within the larger world of the ship. They ate, bunked, and spent their off-duty time only with each other. The sailors, who they looked down upon as plain workmen, disliked them in return. Marines, they said, were ignorant landlubbers. Whenever a seaman said something stupid, he was told to "Go tell it to the marines," who'd believe anything.

During battle, marines manned the ship's fighting tops, tiny platforms high up on the masts used as sniper posts. The marines worked in three- or four-man teams: one sharpshooter and the assistants who kept him supplied with loaded muskets. As the ships drew to musket range, sharpshooters picked off targets on the enemy's decks. Their favorite targets were officers and the sailing master, without whom the vessel couldn't be maneuvered. Lord Nelson was shot in the back by a French sniper at Trafalgar.

The moment the ships collided, other marines, stationed on deck, threw small, sharp-pointed anchors called grapnels across the enemy's deck rails to bind the vessels together. "Boarders away!" shouted the lieutenants, sending marines and sailors swarming over the rails onto the enemy's deck.

In boarding, it was every man for himself. Immediately the battle became a deadly free-for-all with pistols, swords, tomahawks, and short spears called boarding pikes. Boarders sometimes wore high top hats of stiff leather to protect the top of the head. United States Marines are still called "leathernecks," from the old custom of wearing high leather collars to protect their necks from sword slashes.

A ship surrendered when its commander "struck," that is, ordered the flag to be hauled down. The captured vessel was then taken in tow and sold as a prize of war. The money it brought was shared by the victorious ship's officers and crew. Captured crewmen were usually exchanged or freed after promising not to fight for the rest of the war.

*   *   *

Great Britain in 1812 was mistress of the seas. The Royal Navy was not simply large, it outnumbered the navies of any other two countries combined. Altogether its one thousand forty-eight warships mounted twenty-eight thousand cannon and were manned by one hundred fifty-eight thousand seamen. Nearly half of this fleet was made up of ships-of-the-line and frigates.

The Royal Navy was a winner. During fourteen years of war, it had taught the British people to expect victories at sea as regularly as sunrise and sunset. Out of four hundred fleet and single-ship actions, His Majesty's seamen had lost exactly two. And these losses were due to accident or to a small vessel being trapped by a French frigate. But never once during this whole time did an enemy defeat a British ship of the same class.

The Royal Navy was a Goliath, compared to the Americans' David. The entire United States Navy, with its sixteen warships, four hundred forty-two guns, and five thousand men, was smaller than most British squadrons. Indeed, the British had more fighting ships that our navy had guns. When war came, Royal Navy officers joked about the American ships, calling them "bundles of pine boards" with bits of striped rag floating over them.

Yet, like little David, the United States Navy was stronger than it seemed. Its officers were young and vigorous, veterans of the recent war with the Barbary pirates of North Africa. Although small as wars go, this conflict, which lasted on and off from 1801 to 1805, gave the Navy's officers valuable experience.

The United States Navy was built by a pennypinching government that couldn't afford the mighty ships of the line favored in Europe. The service, therefore, decided to concentrate on quality rather than quantity. The heart of the navy was its seven frigates: *Constitution*, *United States*, *President*, *Constellation*, *Congress*, *Chesapeake*, *Essex*. These were no ordinary frigates. Joshua Humphreys, a Philadelphia shipbuilder, had designed three of them — *Constitution*, *United States*, *President* — as super-frigates, the best of their class anywhere in the world.

"Old Ironsides" crashing through the waves under full sail.

Take, for example, *Constitution*, the most famous warship in American history. *Constitution* was built larger and
heavier than other frigates. She measured two hundred four
feet from stem to stern and was forty-three feet wide. Her
one thousand five hundred and seventy-six tons were made
up of the finest materials the country could offer. Every state
from Maine to Georgia sent wood: live oak, red cedar, pitch
pine, locust. The fir for her masts came from the tall timber

of the Northwest Territory. Her iron spikes and anchors were manufactured in New England. Paul Revere made the copper bolts and sheeting for her bottom; copper prevented sea worms from tunneling into the wood.

Big as she was, *Constitution* was built for speed and easy handling. Her long, clean lines allowed her to knife through the waves. Towering masts carried an acre of canvas to catch every breath of wind.

Constitution was as deadly as she was beautiful. Although designed for forty-four guns, she and her two sisters actually carried fifty-four, including twenty-two smashers. No British warship, including ships of the line, had so many carronades for close combat.

The men behind those guns were also the best. The navy trained its seamen, of whom one in six was a free Negro, to razor-sharp perfection. Unlike British crews, who seldom practiced gunnery more than once a year, Americans drilled at rapid loading and target shooting whenever possible. Gunners became so familiar with their weapons that they gave them pet names like "Brother Jonathan," "Raging Eagle," "Spitfire," "Jumping Billy," "Yankee Protection," "Mad Anthony," "Liberty Forever," "Liberty or Death," "United Tars," "Sweetheart," and "Willful Murder."

Warships often flew a banner under the Stars and Stripes that read "Free Trade and Sailors' Rights." This was no empty slogan, but something each crewman felt very strongly about. Many had been impressed and had the scars on their backs to prove it. Every seaman knew someone who was serving Great Britain against his will. If war came, sailors and officers expected the tiny navy to teach Great Britain some painful lessons.

*   *   *

The first lesson was given by a rosy-cheeked, pot-bellied little man from Connecticut. Isaac Hull, born in 1773, was the nephew and adopted son of General William Hull. He went to sea at fourteen as a cabin boy on a merchant vessel, joined the navy in his early twenties, and rose through the ranks to command *Constitution*.

On the afternoon of July 17, 1812, Captain Hull was cruising off Egg Harbor, New Jersey, when he sighted five warships on the horizon. The navy's war plans, he knew, called for sending ships to sea singly or in small groups to protect American and destroy enemy merchantmen. Hull, mistaking these ships for a squadron that had sailed from Chesapeake Bay the week before, took off after them. *Constitution* was catching up when the sun set, plunging the sea into inky blackness. Hull set out signal lanterns, but received no reply. Puzzled, he went to bed.

His question was answered at daybreak. *Constitution* lay at the center of a horseshoe formed by four British frigates and a ship-of-the-line — enough gunpowder to reduce her to splinters in minutes. Hull grabbed his brass speaking trumpet and bellowed orders. Sailors scurried up the rope ladders to the yard arms that carried the sails. A cloud of canvas blossomed, sending *Constitution* forward at top speed.

Hunters and hunted were in a life-and-death race until the wind suddenly slowed, then stopped altogether. And there they sat, bobbing about and staring at each other across three miles of smooth water.

Hull knew that *Constitution* was a goner unless he could increase the distance before the wind came up again. If *Constitution* couldn't carry her crew to safety, they'd have to carry, or, rather, pull her out of danger. Few men could match Isaac Hull's seamanship. Thinking quickly, he had rowboats lowered and attached by heavy cables to the frigate's bow. The sailors in the rowboats then bent their backs and began to row. The cables stiffened. Slowly, slowly, fifteen hundred tons of warship began to move. It was agony for the rowers, for each pull at the oars pulled at their muscles as well. Blisters formed on their hands, then burst. Yet their efforts seemed wasted, for the British were gaining. They, too, sent out rowers; but instead of trying to move the whole squadron, all their rowers concentrated on towing a single frigate.

Hull tried another trick. Every piece of heavy cable aboard *Constitution* was spliced together into a mile-long strand. One end of the line was attached to the ship, the other end to a kedge, or small anchor, which was loaded into a rowboat. The kedge was then carried ahead and dropped into the water, catching on the muddy bottom. *Constitution*'s crew gave a heave-ho on the line and pulled the ship forward. By repeated kedging and hauling *Constitution* gradually pulled away from her pursuers.

Again the British copied Hull. And again they slowly closed the distance. The chase went on like this for two awful days and nights. A few hundred yards more and the enemy would be able to open fire with his long guns.

Fortunately, nature came to *Constitution*'s rescue on the afternoon of the third day. The eastern sky darkened and Hull could see a rain squall dancing along the water in the distance, heading his way. He sent crewmen up the masts to take in the sails as if they were preparing to ride out a hurricane. As he expected, the British played copycat again.

As soon as the squall hit, hiding the frigate behind sheets of rain, Hull's men unfurled the sails. *Constitution* shot forward, picking up her rowboats as she went by. The British, their sails furled and unable to see into the squall, were left far behind.

Constitution made for Boston, where she was welcomed by brass bands and cheering crowds. Isaac Hull had won America's first sea victory of the war. And, except for broken blisters, a completely bloodless one. His next meeting with the enemy, however, would be different.

Hull stayed in Boston only long enough to load fresh supplies and let his crew work the kinks out of their muscles. On August 2, *Constitution* put to sea and headed north in search of enemy targets. Hull especially wanted to find the thirty-eight-gun *Guerrière*, one of the most hated vessels in the Royal Navy. For years she had shadowed American harbors, stopping ships and impressing seamen. Her defeat would cheer the nation more than nearly any other victory.

Hull already knew *Guerrière* and her captain, James R. Dacres. The two officers had met once during a party ashore. Although they knew that war was coming, they chatted politely.

"Well," said Hull, smiling, "you must take good care of that ship of yours, if ever I catch her in *Constitution*."

Dacres laughed and offered to bet money that his *Guerrière* would easily turn out to be the winner.

"No," said Hull, the smile gone from his face, "I'll bet no money on it. But I will bet you a hat that *Constitution* comes out victorious."

"Done," replied Dacres, and they shook hands on the bet.

They met again on a blustery day in the Atlantic two hundred miles east of Halifax, Nova Scotia. It was August 19, 1812, three days after General William Hull's surrender of Fort Detroit.

Constitution had just come over the horizon when Dacres handed his spyglass to William Orne, skipper of a Massachusetts merchantman captured the previous day. "What do you make of her?" Dacres asked.

"One of our frigates," Orne replied.

Dacres disagreed. "He comes on rather too boldly for an American. I would say a Dutchman. However, the better he behaves the more honor we shall gain by taking him." The Englishman was still sure of victory when the stranger came closer and he recognized her as Hull's ship.

Each frigate prepared for action in exactly the same way. Drummer boys rapped out long, urgent rolls to call the crews to battle stations. Instantly the sound of bare feet slapping on wood came from every corner of the vessel. Gunners opened the gun ports and stood beside their loaded weapons with smoking matches. Marine snipers went aloft, while others stood behind the gunners with cocked muskets, ready to shoot anyone who left his post. Powder monkeys brought cartridges from the magazine, then spread sand along the decks; sand prevented men from slipping when the decks became slick with blood.

The frigates' surgeons and their assistants were also busy. Spare spaces belowdecks were cleared and set up as temporary hospitals with old sails spread on the raw planks as beds for the wounded. Tables were moved beneath lanterns, each having an assortment of knives, saws, scissors, needles, and thread arranged along one corner. Not all wounded, though, would see a surgeon. Those who were so badly wounded that they couldn't live would be thrown overboard to end their suffering and prevent their screams from spreading panic among their comrades. The dead were tossed into the sea as soon as they fell so as not to clutter the narrow decks.

Constitution and *Guerrière* advanced boldly, their battle flags whipping against the blue sky. The wind howled, kicking up foamy whitecaps. Ropes vibrated, making an eerie humming sound. Masts creaked under the weight of full-bellied sails. It wouldn't be long now.

Men watched and listened and thought their private thoughts. Everyone knew what to expect if his luck ran out, and was afraid. Some made deals: "If I'm killed, you can have my things; if you're killed, I'll take yours." They were also afraid of being afraid, of letting down their shipmates and losing their self-respect.

Captain Dacres opened the battle by ordering a half turn and firing a cannon to test the range.

Guerrière's port (left) side belched a sheet of flame as every gun fired at once. Most of the heavy balls, however, fell short or flew harmlessly through *Constitution*'s sails. A few struck her side, but rolled into the sea without breaking through the thick oak. "Her sides are made of iron!" a Yankee tar cried. The phrase passed from mouth to mouth throughout the frigate. From then on *Constitution* would be known by her more famous nickname of "Old Ironsides."

Meanwhile, *Guerrière*'s crew worked their guns furiously, sending broadside after broadside at the Americans. Captain Hull paced the quarterdeck, his chubby fingers knotted behind his back, watching the action with keen interest. Except for firing a bow gun now and then, and ordering the sailing master to weave a little to starboard or port, Hull stuck to his course without opening fire.

Constitution's gunners were beginning to wonder about their captain. Old Ironsides' sides were really made of wood, and some shots were breaking through. If she came any closer, *Guerrière* would blast her to driftwood without suffering a scratch to her black and yellow sides.

Hull still paced the quarter-deck. Canister shot rattled through the overhead rigging, too close for comfort. "Shall we open fire, sir?" a lieutenant asked. "Not yet sir, not yet. I will give the order, sir," the captain snapped.

Minutes passed. An eighteen-pound ball hit two men at a gun, killing them instantly and splattering pieces of flesh across the deck. The gunners nearby looked at the pools of blood, then at each other.

The lieutenant looked at Hull. "Not yet, sir, not yet," the captain repeated. Isaac Hull knew the value of patience. He was willing to let the enemy pepper away with his long guns in order to get close enough to use his smashers.

Closer. Closer they came. A hundred yards. *Constitution* mounted a wave, then slid down the other side. Fifty yards. She was nearly alongside *Guerrière*.

"Now, boys, pour it into them!" Hull shouted, motioning with such energy that his skintight breeches split down the center. Everyone was too busy or too excited to notice the captain's bare bottom gleaming in the sunlight.

Constitution's full broadside went off in an earsplitting clap of thunder. Across the way, *Guerrière*'s crew heard the crash and felt their ship shudder as the cannonballs struck. The next moment mangled seamen were being carried down to the surgeons, who soon had more work than they could handle.

Again and again *Constitution*'s broadsides tore into the enemy hull, the body of the ship. "Hull her, boys! Hull her!" the captain shouted at the top of his voice. The gunners took up the cry, chanting "Hull her! Hull her!" after each shot.

The iron monsters on both vessels sprang to life with a flash and a roar. Each time a gun captain brought down his match, the powder in the touchhole gave a sharp WHUFF, squirting a jet of flame upward. The cannon roared and leaped back in recoil; anyone not fast enough to get out of the way might have legs broken. The concussion set off shockwaves that struck the ears like a hard fist; a gunner who forgot to tie a bandanna around his head became permanently deaf.

Smoke built up faster than it could escape through the gun ports, filling the decks with a dense, grayish haze. Men saw each other as moving shadows; they loaded the guns by touch. Smoke made them cough and sneeze; their eyes stung and tears flowed. Particles of unburned gunpowder clung to their bodies, burning them black as coal. The men lost track of time.

Guerrière was being shot to pieces. Carronade balls broke through her sides. Showers of jagged splinters, each a foot long, whizzed through the air. Chunks of wood rained down from the rigging. Cut chains and ropes lashed about wildly. She fought on.

A hail of grape shot brought down *Guerrière*'s mizzen, or third, mast, hurling the topmen into the sea. But instead of falling clear, the wreckage hung over the rear of the frigate, spinning her around like a huge rudder. Seeing this, Hull eased *Constitution* across the British ship's bow, raking her with broadsides from stem to stern.

Suddenly the wounded ship lurched forward and jabbed her bowsprit over the American's deck. Marines in the fighting tops of both vessels blazed away with muskets at close range. It was impossible to miss. Deckmen were dropping all around when the cry "Boarders away!" rose above the din of battle. Both captains had the same idea at once. Boarders rushed forward, only to be turned back when a swell separated the ships a moment later.

As they drew apart, Hull's gunners fired another raking broadside from only a few feet away. *Guerrière*'s foremast tottered for a few seconds then collapsed as if felled by loggers, snapping the mainmast as it went. Without sails to steady her, the proud frigate rolled crazily in the waves. She lay helpless, a shattered wreck, completely out of control, with water pouring through the gun ports each time she dipped into the waves.

Constitution moved off a short distance for minor repairs before taking up a raking position again. Yet her guns remained silent. Hull's intention wasn't to fire, only to show

The fight between the **Constitution** and the **Guerrière**. The American ship has just shot down the enemy's sails, making the frigate a helpless wreck, drifting out of control.

Dacres that he could blast *Guerrière* at will. Seeing this, the Englishman swallowed his pride and hauled down his colors from the mainmast's stump.

A small miracle began to take place the moment *Guerrière* surrendered. Men who had risked their lives to harm the enemy suddenly became kind and considerate. All through the night, as *Guerrière* filled with water, her wounded were transferred to *Constitution*. The American seamen not only fed them and cared for their wounds, but rowed back and forth in the high seas to save their personal belongings. Not once did an American insult a prisoner or gloat over his defeat.

Dacres, who had been wounded, climbed aboard *Constitution* to surrender. "Dacres, give me your hand. I know you are hurt," said Hull.

The Englishman took a deep breath and held out his sword as a sign of surrender. "No, no, Captain," said Hull, raising his hands as if to push the blade away. "I will not take a sword from one who knows so well how to use it. But I will trouble you for that hat." Isaac Hull never forgot a promise or a bet.

The last prisoners were taken off *Guerrière* next morning. As the boats pulled away, torches were flung onto the sinking ship. Americans and Englishmen watched, hypnotized, until the fire reached the magazine and she disappeared in a shattering explosion.

A few days later, *Constitution* swept into Boston harbor with a British battleflag floating beneath the Stars and Stripes. The city went wild with joy, for Americans needed something to cheer about after the defeat of General William Hull. His seafaring nephew had saved the Hull family's reputation.

But the price had been high. In less than a half hour the British had lost twenty-three killed and fifty-six wounded; the Americans had seven dead and seven hurt. In his official report of the battle, Hull singled out *Constitution*'s Negro seamen for special commendation: "I never had any better fighters . . . they stripped to the waist and fought like devils . . . utterly insensible to danger and possessed with a determination to outfight white sailors."

A grateful Congress voted fifty thousand dollars for *Constitution*'s crew in place of the prize money lost when *Guerrière* blew up. Hull received a gold medal and a promotion to commander of the Boston Navy Yard, a post he held for many years. He never fought again.

*   *   *

Guerrière's loss was only the beginning of the Royal Navy's troubles. Hull's victory inspired, and challenged, other American skippers. What he had done, they could do better — or that's what they told themselves. They'd surely *try* to do better.

The next test came in the West Indies on October 18, 1812. The sloop *Wasp*, Captain Jacob Jones, had been raiding Jamaica-bound merchantmen when she met the British sloop *Frolic*. Both vessels were evenly matched, the Englishman with twenty guns to the American's nineteen. Yet an hour's fighting once again proved the value of American seamanship and gunnery. Although badly damaged, *Wasp* was able to put *Frolic* out of action, killing ninety of her one hundred and seven crewmen. Unfortunately, *Wasp*'s damage prevented her escaping from a ship of the line that came along later in the day.

Wasp's loss was soon avenged by a Yankee daredevil named Stephen Decatur. Born in Maryland in 1779, Decatur was a sickly child. At the age of eight he caught the whooping cough and might have died had his father, a merchant

John Bull, symbol of Great Britain, is humiliated and helpless when attacked by America's **Wasp** and **Hornet**, deadly warships.

John Bull stung to agony by the Wasp *and* Hornet.

captain, not taken him on a long voyage. The clean salt air revived the youngster and he decided to make a career of the sea. Decatur joined the navy as a teenager, becoming in time captain of the forty-four-gun frigate *United States*, "Old Ironsides' " sister ship.

"God bless him; he has a soul to save," grizzled old seamen said, touching their caps as the young captain walked by on his rounds. Decatur was a natural leader, who earned his crew's loyalty. Actually, the band of tattooed roughnecks he commanded loved him as a brother.

Seamen and officers knew that Decatur was one of them. He never *sent* them into danger; he *led* them. An insult to any of them was an insult to him.

A brutal officer once kicked a seaman in the face for misunderstanding an order. The sailor ran to the quarterdeck to show Decatur his swollen eye and demand justice. The captain dropped everything and had the bugler sound assembly. As everyone looked on in silence, Decatur gave the guilty officer a tonguelashing that made his cheeks flush with shame. Decatur had only to lead and the men of *United States* would follow him anywhere, no questions asked.

He took them to the Canary Islands off the west coast of Africa to hunt British merchantmen homeward bound from the Far East with cargoes of silks and spices. There, on October 25, 1812, they were sighted by the enemy. The thirty-eight-gun frigate *Macedonian* was commanded by Captain John S. Carden, a good sailor with an evil reputation. Carden ruled his vessel with "whip law." Men died aboard *Macedonian* because he insisted they be whipped even though the surgeon said they couldn't take so much punishment all at once.

Carden ordered the drummers to sound battle stations the moment the Americans hove into view. It so happened that *Macedonian* had several impressed New Englanders aboard. When they learned who they'd be fighting, they sent seaman John Card to beg the captain not to make them fire on their own flag. Captain Dacres also had had Americans aboard *Guerrière*, but sent them below rather than force them to fight. Carden, however, ordered them back to their

Captain Stephen Decatur of the United States. *This is an engraving of a portrait by Alonzo Chappel.*

posts, threatening to shoot the first man who bothered him again. A half-hour later John Card lay dead, cut down by American grape shot.

Decatur, meanwhile, had also sent his crew to battle stations. Among them was a ten-year-old boy named Jack

Creamer. Although everyone knew he was below the legal age to serve on a warship, he was taken aboard anyhow to do odd jobs. The call to battle stations seemed to worry the youngster. His friends noticed his expression and asked if he was afraid. Afraid! Certainly not; not he, Jack Creamer. But he had to see the captain immediately.

An officer marched him up to the quarterdeck, where he stood, hat in hand, waiting for Decatur to notice him.

"Well, Jack, what do you want?" said Decatur cheerily.

"Captain," the youngster answered, "will you please have my name put down on the muster roll?" He wanted to be made officially a member of the crew.

"Why, what for, my lad?"

Drawing himself up to his full height, the boy said firmly, "So that I can draw my share of the prize money when we beat that Britisher, sir."

Decatur, who admired courage in anyone, chuckled and gave the order, making Jack the youngest ever to serve as a crewman aboard an American warship.

Jack's name had hardly been entered on the muster roll when the frigates began approaching each other on a long, gradual course, like the blades of a scissor slowly closing. The Englishmen were impressed by the American captain's seamanship, whoever he was; they didn't know they were up against Decatur in the *United States* until after the battle.

Macedonian's officers scanned the enemy through their spyglasses. They caught glimpses through the open ports of gun crews standing by, lighted matches at the ready. On the quarter-deck they saw American officers looking them over with equal interest. One man didn't seem to belong. He wore no uniform, only a plain brown suit with a tattered straw hat — Decatur. A veteran British gunner turned to a shipmate and said loud enough for everyone to hear: "It's no fool of a seaman handling that ship. We've got hot work ahead of us."

The frigates drew within range and began firing with their long guns. Instead of hoisting more sail to speed up, Decatur shouted for the topmen to reduce the spread of canvas. *United States* slowed down until she lay practically still in the water. She was a perfect target, but also a solid gun platform, allowing the gunners to take careful aim. Decatur, like Hull, was a patient man, willing to take punishment until absolutely the right moment to open fire. When that moment came, he gave the signal to cut loose with every gun.

Both vessels lay broadside and banged away as rapidly as the crews could reload. On *Macedonian*'s quarterdeck, Carden and his officers saw the American shrouded in clouds of smoke. Bursts of flame flashed within the clouds, giving them an orange-red glow. "She's on fire!" an officer shouted. The British gunners, thinking the battle over, cheered.

But they cheered too soon, for *United States* wasn't burning. Decatur had trained his crew to fire three broadsides in the time it took others to fire two. The "fire" the English officers saw was really the flashes of broadsides coming their way.

We know what happened next because Samuel Leech, a powder monkey aboard *Macedonian*, later wrote a book about his experiences. Leech was on the main deck when a strange noise, like the tearing of sails, came from overhead. This was the sound of cannonballs flying through the air at terrific speed. "By and by I heard the shot strike the sides of our ship. It was like some awfully tremendous thunderstorm, whose deafening roar is attended by incessant streaks of lightning, carrying death in every flash." A storm of fire and iron blew across the warship's decks. The men on the quarterdeck heard a sharp crack overhead and, looking up, saw the mizzenmast collapsing on them.

Macedonian became a floating slaughterhouse, a scene of unimaginable terror. The young powder monkeys were nearly all wounded or killed in the first minutes of action. One had his leg carried away by a cannon shot, while another was hit in the ankle by grape shot. A third was rushing to his gun when the cartridge he carried exploded in his face. As he raised both hands, as if begging for the pain to go away, a cannonball cut him in half.

Captain Carden now made his last mistake of the

battle. Instead of keeping his distance and depending on his long guns, he decided to rush in as quickly as possible to board the American. As *Macedonian* bore in, Decatur swerved, cut in front, and fired a stream of raking broadsides.

Macedonian seemed to fly apart. Down came her remaining masts in a tangle of rope and wood. Her crew was knocked over like tenpins. A ball flew through one of the gun ports and wiped out the entire gun crew. A man from the next crew ran over and frantically began to turn over the bodies, searching for his best friend. He found him and burst into tears. Kneeling, he cradled the body in his arms and cried, "Oh, God! Tom! Tom! Tom!" A lieutenant saw him and shouted, "Hang your prayers over that thing! Overboard with it and down to your gun!" The order was obeyed and the heartbroken sailor returned to his post.

Samuel Leech remembered a fellow named John who had been put aboard *Macedonian* as punishment for something he had done on another ship. The last time he saw John they were rushing him belowdecks to the surgeon. "I distinctly heard the large drops of blood falling pat-pat-pat on the deck. The wound was mortal."

Decatur, in the meantime, turned *United States* into broken figure eights to give the guns on the unengaged side a chance at the enemy while the others were reloaded. Suddenly he ordered "Cease fire!"

At first the silence surprised the Englishmen. Then the smoke clouds lifted, revealing *United States* holding a raking position off their stern. Decatur had only to give the command and they'd be blown sky-high. Carden immediately surrendered.

A boarding party under Lieutenant Nicholson was sent to take possession of the prize. The Americans couldn't believe their eyes when they clambered aboard the shattered hulk. Dead and wounded lay everywhere. Sailors wandered about, dazed and exhausted. They met a boy who was crying: his only friend, an older, fatherly man, had been killed. The passageways were crowded with wounded waiting their turn on the surgeon's table.

"How do you do?" asked Lieutenant Nicholson, looking over the surgeon's shoulder.

The gray-haired man turned from his work and replied: "I have enough to do. You fellows have made wretched work for us with your guns."

"Would you like some of our surgeons to help you?" said the lieutenant.

The Englishman's mouth sagged. " I would think they have enough work tending to your own wounded."

Nicholson's answer fell like a ton of bricks: "Oh, no. There were only seven, and their injuries were dressed long ago." When the casualties were counted, it was found that the Americans had five dead and seven wounded, compared to *Macedonian*'s six killed and sixty-eight wounded.

Macedonian was a rich prize. After repairing her worst damage at sea, Decatur had her sailed across the Atlantic to New London, Connecticut, where she became a vessel of the United States Navy.

Jack Creamer had his share of the prize money. When Decatur asked what he'd do with so much money, maybe as much as two hundred dollars, Jack's eyes lit up and he sang his answer. "Please, sir, I'll send half of it to my mother; and the rest will get me a bit of schooling." Jack got his "bit of schooling" and Decatur's friendship beside. He was studying to become a naval officer when he accidentally drowned. A seaman in those days had to know how to handle a ship, not how to swim; most, in fact, couldn't swim a stroke. Samuel Leech, however, enlisted in the United States Navy and lived to a ripe old age.

*　　*　　*

The American winning streak continued throughout the year 1812. The nation received a late Christmas present when, on the afternoon of December 29, *Constitution*, now commanded by Captain William Bainbridge, met the thirty-eight-gun frigate *Java* off the coast of Brazil. During the two-hour battle that followed, the Britisher had one hundred fifty killed and wounded to the American's thirty-four. *Java* took such a pounding that she was useless as a prize and had to be burned.

The tiny United States Navy had twisted the British lion's tail, making it roar in shame and pain. News of *Java*'s loss drew a long article from *The Times* newspaper of London on March 20, 1813:

> The public will learn . . . that a third British frigate has struck to an American. . . . This is an occurrence that calls for serious reflection — this, and the fact that . . . upward of five hundred British vessels (have been) captured in seven months by the Americans. Five hundred merchant-men and three frigates? Can these statements be true? Can the English people hear them unmoved? Any one who would have predicted such a result of an American war this time last year would have been treated as a madman or a traitor. He would have been told . . . that the American flag would have been swept from the seas, the contemptible navy of the United States annihilated, and her marine arsenals rendered a heap of ruins. Yet down to this moment not a single American frigate has struck her flag.

Orders flew from the Admiralty, the Royal Navy's headquarters in London, to all units at sea. Warship commanders were told to travel in pairs and never engage America's super-frigates unless success seemed certain. Merchantmen were to sail in large convoys escorted by frigates and other fighting vessels. And, most important of all, squadrons were taken off the French blockade and sent to blockade the United States. By the spring of 1813, therefore, America's ports were shut tight. The nation's seagoing trade came to a standstill, its proud frigates resting at dockside, safe behind powerful shore batteries but now useless in the war effort.

The British had their revenge on June 1, 1813, when H.M.S. *Shannon* defeated USS *Chesapeake* in the last single-frigate action of the war. Although closely matched in size and firepower, these thirty-eight-gun frigates were worlds apart in their readiness for battle. *Chesapeake* was anchored in the Boston Navy Yard, having just taken on a new commander and crew. Captain James Lawrence was an experienced officer who had been given *Chesapeake* as a reward for past service. As with any captain taking over a new vessel, Lawrence needed time to learn her little tricks, for no two ships sail exactly alike. He didn't have that time. Nor did he have time to hammer his crew into a fighting team. *Chesapeake*'s crew was made up of men from different vessels who had never served together. Many feared the ship, believing her jinxed ever since a run-in with the British ship *Leopard* six years earlier.

Chesapeake faced one of the Royal Navy's finest frigates. A warship is only as good as her captain, and Philip Bowes Vere Broke was the best. Unlike his fellow captains, Broke trained his men at gunnery twice a week, weather permitting. His gunners drilled at rapid loading and firing until they became as good as any crew in the world. The gun crew with the highest score at target practice received a prize of a pound of tobacco paid for out of the captain's own pocket.

Broke wasn't satisfied with seeing *Chesapeake*'s tall, slender masts standing out against the distant shoreline. One day he sent Lawrence a written challenge to meet him for a ship-to-ship duel. The American, he promised, needn't worry about being outnumbered, as he had sent away his escorting frigate. The captains should meet like knights of the Middle Ages to see which commander and vessel was best.

"She's coming out!" a lookout shouted from *Shannon*'s mainmast. There, to the west, *Chesapeake* was gliding out to sea on the tide under full sail. Thousands of Bostonians lined the shore, while dozens of crowded pleasure boats followed behind, eager to see a naval battle. They were disappointed, however, because the captains preferred to fight on the high seas, free from distraction. Only watchers on the far-off heights of Salem caught glimpses of the gunflashes through their spyglasses.

The frigates went to work immediately. No fancy sailing. No cutting and dodging. They simply came within pistol shot, broadside to broadside, and blazed away.

The training Broke had given his crew soon paid off. The British fired faster and more accurately than their

"Don't give up the ship." Captain James Lawrence issues his last command as he is carried below decks, dying, during the battle between the **Chesapeake** and **Shannon**.

enemy. Within minutes, *Chesapeake*'s rigging was in shreds, making it impossible to keep her under control. Lawrence, in the thick of the fight, stood his ground even though a musket ball tore through his leg. He was shouting encouragement to his men when another bullet hit him in the chest; this time some deckhands carried him below, dying. His last order has been passed down to generation after generation of United States Navy men: *"Don't give up the ship!"*

But it was already too late for *Chesapeake*. Minutes later, Broke led a boarding party onto her deck for the final assault. A wild, every-man-for-himself brawl followed in which men shot, stabbed, even bit, each other. Broke took a sword cut in the head and went down with an American tar on top of him. At that moment a British marine rushed up and, mistaking Broke for a Yankee officer, was about to run him through when he cried, "Poh! Poh! You fool! Don't you know your captain?" The marine instantly changed the direction of the blow. Broke fainted from loss of blood, awakening to find himself a national hero.

After three losses in frigate actions, the Royal Navy could finally point to a victory. When *Shannon*'s news reached England, the country went wild with joy, as if Napoleon himself had been overthrown. The giant guns in the Tower of London boomed out in celebration. Broke was made a nobleman and, in time, an admiral as well. *Chesapeake* became a vessel of the Royal Navy, in which she served honorably for many years.

*   *   *

At the very moment Broke's marines stormed *Chesapeake*, the U.S.S. *Essex* was roaming the Pacific on a history-making voyage. The thirty-two-gun vessel, smallest frigate in the United States Navy, was commanded by Captain David Porter, a sour-faced Bostonian with a grudge against the Royal Navy. Born in 1780, Porter learned about impressment the hard way. As a lad of sixteen he fought in a bloody battle to drive a British impressment detail off his father's cargo ship in the West Indies. Next year, on his second voyage, Porter was taken off another vessel at gunpoint and hustled aboard a British frigate. The frigate captain was astonished to find that he had captured a lion, not a lamb. Porter not only refused to obey orders, he encouraged other Americans aboard to disobey. The captain ordered him whipped, but the night before the order was to be carried out he slipped overboard, into shark-infested waters, and was rescued by a Danish vessel in the nick of time. Impressed a second time, he could only escape after several months of bad treatment for refusing to serve under any flag except that of the United States.

Free again, the youngster, by now as hard as nails, joined the navy, rising to captain's rank when the War of 1812 began. Porter ran a "tight ship." He trained *Essex*'s crew to be ready for any emergency. At any hour of the night he sounded the most dreaded alarm: "Fire!" Or he had the bugler sound "Repel Boarders!" when least expected. Laggards had to make do on bread and water for a week; repeated offenders cooled their heels in the brig, the ship's prison room, a cold, damp place favored by rats. Before long no emergency, real or staged, could faze *Essex*'s crew.

They had to be alert to carry out the mission Porter planned. The British kept a large whaling fleet in the Pacific Ocean off the western coast of South America. Every year this fleet sent home millions of dollars worth of whale oil, prized as a fuel for lamps. Since no American warship had ever entered the Pacific, the admiralty saw no need to protect the whalers. That was a mistake.

Porter cleared Delaware Bay in October, 1812, and headed for Cape Horn at the southern tip of South America. One day his crew noticed that the sun rose, not on their left, but at their backs; they had rounded Cape Horn and entered the Pacific.

*David Porter led his crew aboard the USS **Essex** on a raid into the Pacific Ocean that destroyed the British whaling industry.*

The Pacific's greeting was anything but "pacific"—peaceful. It was now February, 1813, and the weather grew worse daily. The wind howled, driving the vessel with such force that it seemed the masts would snap. *Essex* mounted thirty-foot waves, dropping suddenly into a watery valley before mounting the next wave. Heavy cabinets skidded across the decks. Men toppled from their hammocks.

The ship passed from one rainstorm to another. The temperature dropped, the cold becoming so intense that the windblown sea spray left red welts wherever it touched unprotected skin.

Essex stank of cold and damp, made all the worse because the cooking fires had to be doused during storms. Only salt meat and moldy flour remained in the food lockers, and these were quickly running out. Men became so desperate for fresh meat that they hunted ship's rats. Rats weren't too bad, eaten raw and cold, so long as you didn't look them in the face. Just when everything seemed lost, *Essex* broke through the storm and headed for Valparaiso, Chile, where Porter rested his crew and bought fresh supplies.

The British whaling fleet was taken completely by surprise. For the next six months Porter cruised the Pacific, capturing enemy ships at will. Every victory made possible the next victory, for his prizes were filled with everything *Essex* needed to remain at sea: paint, rope, tar, anchors, medicines, food.

Most whalers were burned and their crews taken prisoner. When Porter gathered enough prisoners, he put them aboard a captured ship and set them free. One ship, though, was so strongly built that he turned her into an auxiliary warship, *Essex Junior.* So many prizes were taken that he even put one in charge of little Davy Farragut, his adopted twelve-year-old son. The training the youngster received on this voyage served him the rest of his life. David Glasgow Farragut became the first admiral of the United States Navy. During the Civil War, Farragut, now in his sixties, led a fleet into action with the cry, "Damn the torpedoes! Full speed ahead!"

*View of the **Essex** and some of her prizes. From a drawing by Captain Porter.*

Porter's mini-squadron became so troublesome that the admiralty sent three warships under Captain John Hillyar to hunt it down. Hillyar caught up with the Americans during a stopover at Valparaiso, March 22, 1814. Chile was a neutral country, and Porter knew the enemy had no right to come into the harbor after him. He also knew that the enemy outnumbered him six to one in long guns, *Essex* being fitted almost entirely with short-range carronades. Fearing that the two *Essexes* would be battered to pieces if Hillyar decided to violate Chilean neutrality, Porter tried to escape.

Unfortunately, a sudden gust of wind carried away one of *Essex*'s main sails, allowing the British to trap her between the open sea and the shore. For two hours Porter fought an uneven battle. *Essex* was pounded without being able to hit back. Her decks became a shambles of splintered wood, torn rigging, and pieces of human bodies. Fires spread toward the magazines. Of her crew of two hundred fifty-five, all but a hundred lay dead or wounded. At last the captain ordered the code book destroyed and surrendered. *Essex Junior* also struck her colors. But there was nothing to be ashamed of, for during their seventeen-month adventure, Porter and his crew had crippled an important enemy industry and proven that American warships could operate far from their bases for long periods of time.

* * *

The navy, however, did not fight the sea war singlehandedly. In 1812, as in 1776, the United States Government issued a call for privateers. Privateers were not part of the navy or bound by its rules. They were private citizens who used their own ships to wage war on the enemy. Although privateering is outlawed today, for centuries governments issued *letters of marque and reprisal* allowing their citizens to attack enemy shipping in wartime. Without these documents a captured crew could be hung for piracy; with them they were treated as war prisoners. Letters of marque and reprisal were actually invaluable hunting licenses permitting anyone to buy a ship, hire a crew, and keep all profits tax-free. They were worth many times their weight in gold, and the government issued five hundred twenty-six of them during the war with Britain.

The Atlantic coast of the United States was a perfect base for privateers. Hundreds of rivers and creeks empty into the ocean; hundreds of bays and coves are protected from the ocean's breakers — and from prying eyes. And, in time, hundreds of small shipyards sprang up in these out-of-the-way places. They built, not frigates, but a vessel known as the "Baltimore Clipper," named after its birthplace; "clipper" was a slang word for "fast" or "racy."

Even today the Baltimore clippers are considered miracles of the shipbuilder's art. These privateer craft had two main features: ease of handling and speed. Above all *speed*! Speed to catch a merchantman. Speed to attack. Speed to escape. Everything was sacrificed to speed. Their sides were paper-thin; incredibly tall masts were tilted back sharply in order to carry a cloud of canvas. Longer than most vessels, and narrower, clippers were like knife blades slicing through the waves. Their only armament was a single "long tom" (long-range) cannon and some smaller pieces, popguns compared to a warship's guns. A single carronade shot could have blasted most privateers out of the water.

The British had made sure that privateer captains would never have a problem raising crews. By bottling up the American merchant fleet, their lordships of the admiralty had thrown thousands of seafarers out of work. One had only to fire a musket from the upper window of a waterfront tavern in New York, Boston, Salem, Baltimore, and a dozen other places to bring them running. "Come one. Come all. Hard work. Easy money. Lots of it."

Men back from successful cruises strutted about with ten-dollar bills stuck in their hatbands, pockets bulging with coins. A family of five could live comfortably for a month on ten dollars in 1813. Privateering became so profitable that banks gladly lent money to daring sea captains.

The whole watery world became their hunting ground. Wherever British merchantmen sailed, there, too, came American privateersmen hot on their trail. They would strike, loot and disappear until ready to attack again hundreds of miles away.

The full story of the privateers is too long for this book. But a few examples tell a lot. For instance *Rossie* of Baltimore, Joshua Barney commanding, ruined the British sugar trade in the West Indies, returning with over a million dollars in cash and loot. *Leo* and *Lion*, also of Baltimore, took twenty-eight vessels off the coast of Portugal; because of them the British army fighting in Spain couldn't be paid on time. *Rambler* scoured the Indian Ocean, like Captain Kidd a hundred years earlier. *Yankee* returned from Africa with tons of ivory and forty thousand dollars in gold dust. *America* stood off Halifax and, within sight of enemy ships-of-the-line, took a ship worth nearly a million dollars. Jamaica, the old pirate stronghold in the Caribbean, was visited regularly by privateers, who took two hundred ships in a few months. Merchants begged the admiralty for help: "They (the Americans) are becoming so daring as to cut vessels out of harbors, though protected by batteries, and to land and carry off cattle from the plantations. Jamaica is blockaded by their privateers."

Such complaints didn't help, for the Royal Navy had its hands full closer to home. Privateer captains discovered that the richest hunting grounds were off the British Isles themselves. *True-Blooded Yankee* led the way into the Irish Sea between Great Britain and Ireland. Every week, sometimes every night for weeks, the glare of a burning ship acted as a beacon pointing to another privateer's prize.

The all-time king of the privateers was the *Chasseur*, commanded by "Wild" Tom Boyle. *Chasseur*, French for "hunter," prowled the English Channel like a hungry wolf. She led a charmed life. Dozens of times she struck and escaped just as British frigates came over the horizon. Once the twenty-gun *St. Lawrence* caught her by pretending to be a cargo ship. Too bad for *St. Lawrence*. Boyle drove in through the gunsmoke and captured her after a rough-and-tumble sword fight across her deck. He became so bold after this victory that he announced *Chasseur* was blockading the British Isles all by itself.

Only one hundred forty-eight privateers were lost during the war. Some were cornered by frigates operating in packs, others were decoyed by men-of-war masquerading as merchantmen or captured when disabled by storms. Never once, however, was an American privateer run down by an enemy warship in the open sea.

America's privateers took one thousand three hundred and forty-five vessels, and probably others their captains didn't bother to report. As a result, prices in England skyrocketed. Coffee, oranges, sugar, and other goods soared out of reach of ordinary people. The only way to guarantee that an overseas letter reached its destination was to put it on a ship-of-the-line.

The British wondered where it would all end. So did the Americans.

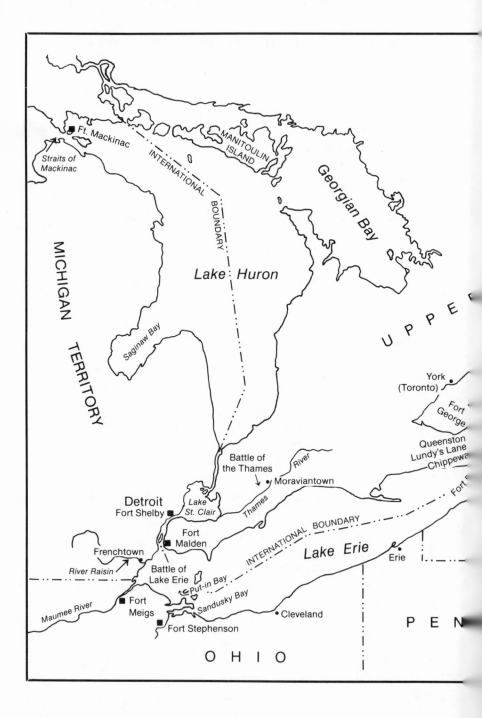

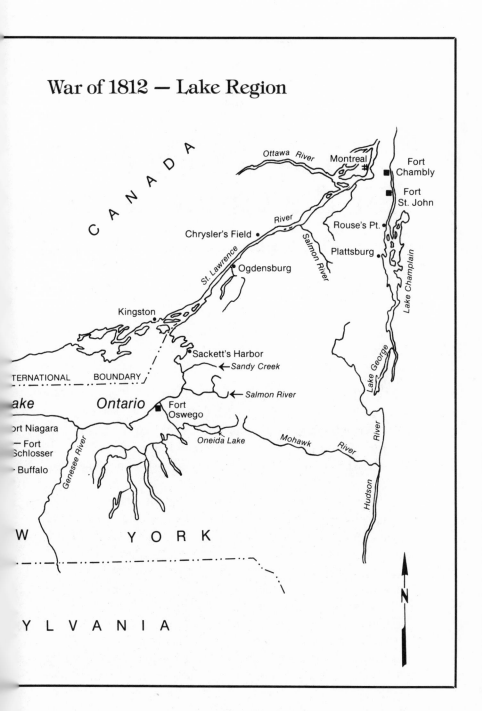

War of 1812 — Lake Region

4

The Struggle for the Great Lakes

William Henry Harrison paced the floor of his tiny office at Fort Meigs. Glad as he was to have news of the navy's frigate victories, his assignment remained as difficult as ever. If anything, the news made him more downhearted. Here it was, June, 1813, and the enemy still controlled the Northwest.

By God, he envied those frigate captains! He'd give anything to have an Old Ironsides on Lake Erie; he'd even settle for a few of those pint-sized privateersmen. For Harrison knew that sea power, or rather lake power, held the key to victory in the Northwest. In order to win on land, he first needed ships to protect his supply line along Lake Erie and prevent supplies reaching the British at Detroit and Fort Malden.

The general's hopes lay with a tall, gawking naval officer of twenty-seven named Oliver Hazard Perry. Born August 23, 1785, at South Kingston, Rhode Island, Perry was another Yankee who grew up with a burning resentment of Great Britain. He always remembered how his father,

Christopher Raymond Perry, a jovial man, became serious when he spoke about the British. The elder Perry captained the *General Greene*, a small warship used for escorting merchantmen. He was guarding a cargo ship when he had to face down an impressment detail by opening his gun ports.

"It is a most surprising thing," shouted the English captain, his face purple with rage, "if a British seventy-four-gun ship cannot search a pitiful little Yankee merchantman."

"By Heaven!" the American answered back. "You shall not do it to the dishonor of my flag." No Englishman set foot aboard the Yankee merchantman that day.

Oliver shipped out with his father and, at the age of fourteen, enlisted in the Navy. He earned quick promotion, becoming a master-commandant, which used to be the rank between lieutenant and captain.

When the War of 1812 began, Perry was in charge of eight gunboats stationed at Newport, Rhode Island. Bold, handsome, a natural leader, he itched for a combat assignment. None came. He felt that while others served with Isaac Hull and Stephen Decatur, he played nursemaid to a flock of overgrown water beetles.

In February, 1813, a few weeks after the River Raisin Massacre, a messenger arrived from Washington with a large brown envelope. Somehow the Navy Department had gotten the idea that Perry was the type of man it needed for a special job. Although he would be under the overall command of Commodore Isaac Chauncey at Sackett's Harbor, New York, Perry was on his own. His orders were short and snappy, like a cannon shot: Hurry to Lake Erie. Build a battle fleet. Defeat the British lake fleet. Period.

Perry started immediately, setting out from Newport in the middle of the harsh New England winter. The roads were blocked with snow as his sleigh sped cross-country bound for Lebanon, Connecticut, where his parents lived in retirement. Time was precious, and he could only stay overnight, but he couldn't go away without saying goodbye.

Next morning, as he was preparing to leave, his thirteen-year-old brother, Alexander, begged to go along. Mother Perry held back. Matthew Calbraith, her middle son, was a lieutenant aboard the *United States*; in years to come he'd lead a fleet into Tokyo harbor to open American trade with Japan. Oliver Hazard, her oldest, was going off to war. And now Alexander, her youngest, wanted to sail into danger with him. She thought for a moment, then decided, sadly. The Perrys had always been fighters, and this was no time to break with family tradition, she thought. She gave her consent and her blessing.

The brothers traveled by sleigh and coach from Lebanon to Albany, New York, where they met Commodore Chauncey and the Newport gunboat men, reassigned to lake duty. Chauncey told Perry that his headquarters would be at Presque Isle (now Erie, Pennsylvania) and sent him on his way.

Perry's party set out on sleds across the frozen wilderness. The temperature dropped to below zero and stayed there. The weak sun did nothing to brighten the gray sky. The sleds glided between mountainous snowdrifts and across frozen streams. All was quiet, save for the pattering of the horses' hooves and the sleds' runners swishing over the snow. The only living things they saw were deer and occasional Indians huddled in furs. It became so lonely that they fired a musket now and then or shouted to break the silence. After two weeks, they arrived at their destination.

Presque Isle lay on the south shore of Lake Erie. The base was nothing but a cleared patch of ground along the lakeshore with four log cabins and a harbor with a sandbar across its mouth; the water here was so shallow that only small vessels could float across without getting stuck. This proved an advantage, for it kept British warships out of the harbor, allowing the Americans to work safe from attack.

Only now did Perry realize the difficulty of his assignment. He found not a fleet, but five half-built ships: two twenty-gun brigs and three smaller craft. But most of the shipwrights, or shipbuilders, were on strike and construction nearly halted. Worse, Perry's command was starved for supplies. Not a coil of rope, anchor, sail, cannon, or even a musket was to be found within a hundred miles. These difficulties only brought out the stubborn streak that ran through the Perry family. Come what may, he'd build that fleet.

Perry spoke to the strikers, appealing to their patriotism and promising better pay. Soon the work was going along as smoothly as ever. There was plenty of timber in the forest — chestnut, white and black oak, pine — to supply the shipwrights. Often a tree cut down in the morning became part of a vessel by afternoon. Since there were no nails, holes had to be bored and planks joined with wooden pegs. Of course the green lumber would warp quickly, twisting out of shape. But that made no difference to Perry; he wasn't building the fleet to last forever, only long enough to defeat the enemy or be blown to bits in a day's fighting.

Supplies began to arrive during the spring. Perry had wagonloads of equipment hauled over muddy wilderness trails from Buffalo, New York, at the lake's eastern end. He personally visited the tiny ironmaking town of Pittsburgh, Pennsylvania, to buy anchors, hoops, bolts, and other hardware.

The Lake Erie fleet was ready by the second week in July, 1813. Its main vessels were the twenty-gun brigs *Lawrence* and *Niagara*. Perry chose *Lawrence* as his flagship, naming it for the heroic James Lawrence, captain of *Chesapeake*, his friend who had died the month before. These vessels, the largest in the squadron, measured one hundred ten feet long by twenty-nine feet wide. Their sister ships were eighty feet long and twenty feet wide, the size of a World War II PT (patrol torpedo) boat. They were joined by several other smaller craft brought up the Niagara River from Lake Ontario.

The British, meanwhile, were busy at Fort Malden. Their naval commander was Captain Robert Barclay, a one-armed veteran who had served with Admiral Nelson at Trafalgar. Barclay's shipyard on the Detroit River had built a small, yet powerful, squadron of fighting vessels. Best of all, his flagship, the twenty-gun *Detroit*, was nearing completion.

Barclay patrolled off Presque Isle, hoping to catch the Americans while they were taking their ships over the sandbar into the open lake. Several times he challenged Perry to come out and fight, but Perry held back, determined to set the time and place of battle himself. Captain Lawrence's defeat had taught him a valuable lesson about accepting challenges when unprepared.

The enemy had the best of the standoff. As long as Barclay's fleet cruised outside Presque Isle harbor, Perry was trapped and the British able to move supplies freely across the lake.

At dawn, July 31, 1813, American sentries peered into the gloom and found the lake empty. The British blockaders had disappeared. "Perry's luck" they whispered among themselves. Barclay, it seems, had lowered his guard only once. Bored with blockade duty, he accepted an invitation to a party given in his honor by some Canadians. He felt sure that the Americans wouldn't be able to do anything in the few days he'd be away.

Perry grabbed his opportunity with both hands. Swiftly, the smaller vessels glided onto the lake and took battle stations outside the harbor. *Lawrence* was moving ahead smartly when the crew felt a tugging beneath their feet and heard a scraping sound. The brig stuck tight in the sandbar's mud. She was a sitting duck.

Perry's skill as a seaman now paid off. To lighten the vessel, he had her guns dismounted and taken ashore. He then had two large airtight floats called "camels" brought to the brig's sides. The camels were flooded and, when they sank, long beams were placed on their decks and run through *Lawrence*'s gun ports. The camels were then pumped out, lifting the ship over the sandbar as they rose, while sailors in rowboats pulled her across with ropes. It all sounds easier than it was. The men worked nonstop for two days and nights, many dropping from exhaustion. They slept where they fell, deaf to the bustling activity around them.

Lawrence came over the sandbar with only minutes to spare. She was riding at anchor, disarmed, when Barclay's squadron reappeared. Perry realized the enemy could blast his ships to smithereens unless he acted immediately. The only thing to do was bluff and hope for the best. Arranging his smaller craft in line-of-battle formation, he sent them ahead with guns blazing. Barclay, who had no intention of taking on *Lawrence* until *Detroit* was ready, made sail for Fort Malden. With the coast cleared, Perry had *Lawrence* rearmed and set camels to work on *Niagara*.

Yet Perry was still unprepared for a big battle. For a whole month he cruised the lake to familiarize his men with their ships and get them used to working with each other. They needed a lot of practice, for the fleet was badly under-manned. Although Perry had about a hundred men from his Newport gunboats and some veterans from Old Ironsides, most were not experienced seamen. He enlisted anyone who'd serve, including farmhands and a Russian who couldn't speak a word of English. One in four was a free Negro who, willing as he might be, knew little about ship handling.

In mid-August Perry joined General Harrison at Sandusky, Ohio, where he was assembling his forces for the coming campaign. The commanders held long meetings, during which they decided that the fleet should be based at Put-in-Bay on an island thirty miles from Fort Malden. Besides giving good advice, Harrison lent Perry the hundred "marines" he needed to round out his fighting strength. These marines were unlike any who had ever set foot on a ship's deck. Kentuckians dressed in buckskins, none had ever been on a ship, and most hadn't even seen one. Yet, when not seasick, they could shoot the whiskers off a squirrel.

From their base at Put-in-Bay, Perry's ships ranged the western part of Lake Erie, bringing enemy traffic to a halt. General Proctor soon felt the pinch at Fort Malden, where fourteen thousand people depended on the army for food. Of these, ten thousand were Tecumseh's warriors and their families. The Indians, who weren't used to rationing supplies to make them go further, ate their fill until only a few days' food remained. No one, not even the great chief, could hold the Indian army together once the food ran out. Ready or not, Captain Barclay had to fight the Americans.

*   *   *

"Sail ho!"

"Enemy approaching!"

At five o'clock in the morning, September 10, 1813, a lookout atop *Lawrence*'s mainmast gave the signal everyone had been expecting for days. Perry, fully clothed, leaped from his bunk and raced topside to see for himself. Out there, in the distance, were six ships with fresh coats of red paint glimmering in the rays of the rising sun. Barclay was coming out to give battle.

Perry was pleased. A spy at Fort Malden had brought news that the British would fight soon. Better still, he had learned the enemy's battle order, which allowed the American commander to make his plans in advance. Those plans called for each ship to fight an enemy vessel of its own class. Thus *Lawrence* would oppose the just-completed *Detroit*; *Niagara*, the *Queen Charlotte*, and so on with the smaller ships.

Although Perry outnumbered the enemy nine ships to six, he knew it would be a tough battle. As usual, the British vessels were armed mostly with long-range guns, the Americans with short-range smashers. Perry told his officers over and over that they must come to grips with the enemy quickly or be shot to pieces from the distance.

"Enemy in sight!"

Perry calmly ordered the fleet to raise anchor, leaving the safety of Put-in-Bay. Topmen scrambled aloft to unfurl the sails, which billowed in the light breeze.

The fleets approached each other slowly, at under three miles an hour, scarcely ruffling the lake's glassy surface. Battle was still several hours away, yet Perry already knew the outcome. As the vessels cleared the harbor, he absent-mindedly glanced skyward. High above, riding an air current, a lone eagle was following the flagship. Perry thought that the bird, the symbol of his country, might be a messenger from Heaven announcing the victory that lay ahead. He squared his shoulders and returned to his tasks, refreshed and confident.

The enemy was six miles away when Perry formed his fleet into two divisions. He'd lead the attack with the *Lawrence* and two gunboats. Lieutenant Jesse D. Elliott would follow in *Niagara*, bringing up the rest of the fleet as quickly as possible.

Perry now showed his seamen their battleflag, which had been sewn secretly weeks before at Presque Isle. It was no ordinary flag, but made of a single piece of blue cloth nine feet square. Its motto was written in white letters a foot high: DON'T GIVE UP THE SHIP.

The young commander stood on a gun carriage and, unrolling the flag, called to his men. "My brave lads, this flag bears the last words of Captain Lawrence. Shall I hoist it?" The answer came in a great shout of "Aye, aye, Sir!" followed by three cheers. As the flag rose, the cheers were taken up by each ship, echoing down the American line until they faded away.

The fleets continued to bear down upon each other slowly, gracefully. At about 10:30 A.M. Perry ordered lunch served, for he reckoned the battle would be well underway when the time came for the regular midday meal. The crews hastily ate their bread, beans, and hard cheese washed down with a mugful of whiskey bought at twenty-five cents a gallon. Many returned to their posts a little fuzzy-headed. It was a good feeling and, while it lasted, took away fear.

The enemy ships were growing larger as Perry passed along the deck to inspect the guns once more and give each crew a final pep talk. Noticing some oldtimers from the *Constitution*, he grinned and said, "I need not say anything to you. *You* know how to beat those fellows." At a nearby gun he saw familiar faces. "Ah!" he exclaimed. "Here are the Newport boys! They will do their duty, I warrant." The inspection completed, all was silence as Perry mounted the steps to the quarter-deck, his command post. The only sounds now were of water lapping against the bows and his shoes crunching on the sanded deck.

The British fleet broke its silence a moment later. A bugle sounded from *Detroit*, followed by cheers from the excited jack tars. At the same time a band struck up "Rule Britannia," a rousing patriotic tune that tells how "Britannia rules the waves." Captain Barclay also knew how to get his men keyed up for the coming ordeal.

The last notes were fading on the breeze when *Detroit* fired a shot to test the range. The twenty-four-pound ball fell into the lake short of its target. Perry promptly signaled his fleet to attack.

Moments later *Detroit* fired a second shot. This time the ball found its mark. There was a shriek of pain as a sailor went down in a cloud of whirring splinters. "Steady, boys, steady!" Perry called to the gunners. They had a long way to go before the carronades could take effect and he didn't want to waste ammunition.

The British certainly weren't wasting ammunition. Every long gun suddenly opened fire with a crash heard fifty miles away. Barclay brought every available gun to bear on *Lawrence*. Victory, he thought, would come automatically if he knocked her out before the Americans' second division joined the battle.

Perry was worried. Although the battle had been going on for fifteen minutes, Lieutenant Elliott's division hadn't come to *Lawrence*'s assistance. If anything, Elliott hung back, deliberately avoiding battle. We'll never know whether he did so from cowardice, stupidity, or anger that Perry and not he had been given command. Whatever the reason, it caused Perry's battle plan to fall apart.

For two hours, as both her gunboat escorts stood by helplessly, *Lawrence* was hammered by concentrated gunfire. Barclay's ships formed a half-circle and poured in broadsides, raking her at will. By the time *Lawrence* came within carronade range, most of her guns were wrecked.

Perry's crew suffered terribly. Men dropped everywhere. Even the wounded weren't safe belowdecks, for cannonballs plowed through the vessel, killing men as they lay on the operating table.

The surgeon did his best, but it could never be enough. Cannon on the deck above roared, sending shivers through the vessel. He continued to work. Blood seeped through cracks in the floorboards overhead, dripping on the wounded and spattering the surgeon from head to foot until he looked like a butcher. And still he worked, automatically, as if his hands knew what to do by themselves.

Oliver Hazard Perry leading his men in battle. An engraving from a portrait by Alonzo Chappel.

At last *Lawrence* came within carronade range and opened fire. It felt good to hit back after taking so much punishment for so long. The buckskin marines high in the rigging were also beginning to pick off individuals on *Detroit*'s deck.

Yet *Lawrence*'s fire could only hurt, not cripple, the enemy. She was fast becoming a defenseless wreck. Much of her canvas was torn to shreds, so that the sails couldn't hold air. Her control cables and steering gear were shot away. Chunks of mast crashed onto the deck, dragging canvas and rope and men with them.

Those who lived through these awful hours would always remember certain incidents. Perry had locked his dog, a small black spaniel, in a cabin to keep him safe. The noise of battle so terrified the animal that its yapping could be heard above the cries of the wounded, even above the gunfire. When a cannonball tore a hole in the cabin's wall, the dog pushed his head through and barked at the enemy. The grimy men forgot the horrors of battle for a moment to laugh at the dog's antics.

Lieutenant John D. Yarnell, *Lawrence*'s second-in-command, had an unconquerable fighting spirit. Rushing up to Perry, he blurted out that all his gunners had been killed and he needed others to take their place. A large splinter had gone through his nose, causing it to swell to the size of a large pickle. Perry grinned, made a joke about the outsize nose and gave him some men. A few minutes later, Yarnell went belowdecks to find more men. He had been wounded again, this time in the scalp. The stuffing from burst mattresses stuck to his bloody face, making him look like a giant owl. Even the serously wounded couldn't help laughing when he appeared. "The devil has come among us! The devil has come among us!" they shouted, tears running down their cheeks, as he raced by.

Perry was everywhere, ordering, encouraging, and lending a helping hand. His life seemed charmed, as if protected by an invisible shield. Two musket balls passed through his hat and his clothing was torn by splinters, leaving him without a scratch. Men were killed standing alongside him. A veteran of Old Ironsides was swearing and shaking his fist at his disabled gun. "Sir, my gun behaves shamefully!" he shouted. Perry was helping him set it up again when a cannonball slammed into the poor man's chest. The commander, though, was unharmed.

Perry remained calm in the midst of the horror around him. Outside, the world was a pandemonium of noise and destruction. But inside, within his own mind and soul, all was peaceful. The worse things became, the cooler he became. It felt as if he wasn't part of the battle, but watching it from a distance.

Only once did he lose his coolness. His brother, Alexander, was standing nearby when Perry saw a twenty-four pounder brush past him. The next moment the youngster fell to the deck in a tangle of rope and netting. In a flash Perry was at his side, holding him, .hugging him, patting him. Luckily Alexander was only stunned. Awakening, he blushed in embarrassment at being coddled by his big brother. "I'm all right, *Sir!*" he said as he snapped a salute and ran to his post.

Lawrence, meanwhile, was going to pieces. When Perry counted his crew after two hours of fighting, he found only seventeen men fit for duty out of the one hundred and three who had gone into battle. One by one the stubby carronades were knocked out and their crews killed. At last, only a single gun remained usable. The gun captain came up to Perry. He was wild-eyed and breathless, shouting "For God's sake, Sir, give me more men!" But Perry had no more men to give. All he could do was stand at the top of the hatchway and call to the operating-room patients: "Can any of the wounded haul on a rope?" The surgeon released three of the least wounded, who limped up the stairs. Minutes passed, and Perry again shouted for more walking wounded, as the first batch were killed. He didn't have to ask for a third group, because the gun was destroyed.

Lawrence suddenly became quiet. The quiet settled over the smoke-filled ship like a soft blanket. The dog stopped barking. Only the low moans of the wounded broke the silence. The crippled vessel wallowed in the water, a helpless wreck. All the British had to do was board her and claim their victory. Perry was beaten, wasn't he?

Not by a long shot. *Lawrence* was beaten, but not her commander or the rest of the American fleet. Looking over his shoulder, Perry saw Lieutenant Elliott's division a half-mile away. "I'll fetch them up!" he hissed through clenched teeth.

In the meantime the British had ceased fire, expecting to see the silent *Lawrence*'s flag lowered any second. Perry, however, had no intention of surrendering. Taking advantage of the lull, he had four sailors lower the gig, a tiny rowboat. As he stepped aboard, he put Lieutenant Yarnell in charge with authority to do what he thought best, hold out or surrender. "If victory is to be gained," he said, "I'll gain it."

The gig was about to push off when a sailor named Hosea Sargent lowered the *Don't give up the ship* banner and tossed it to his commander. Perry was standing upright when it fell across his shoulders, draping him like a rich robe. "Pull!" he ordered the oarsmen.

Perry changes ships during the Battle of Lake Erie.

The gig slid away toward *Niagara*. The clouds of gun-smoke that hugged the water were clearing when Barclay saw Perry and realized what he had in mind. Every gun in the British fleet belched fire. Cannonballs sent fountains of water leaping all around the gig. A grape shot hit its side, whereupon Perry took off his coat to plug the hole. The rowers begged him to sit down, as he was a perfect target. He paid no attention until they rested on the oars and the gig came to a dead stop. Perry was furious, but the men refused to row another inch until he took a seat. He sat, a faint smile creeping over his face.

The gig bumped against the side of *Niagara* fifteen minutes later. It had passed through the fire of the entire enemy fleet without anyone receiving the slightest scratch. Perry's luck held once again.

As Perry climbed up the ship's side, he heard a weak cheer from the *Lawrence*. Her surviving crew had gathered on deck to "help" his rowers with their prayers. A moment later, Yarnell lowered her flag rather than lose lives needlessly. Perry paused on the ladder with tears in his eyes. Then he stepped over *Niagara*'s rail.

Lieutenant Elliott met him with one of the silliest questions in history: "How goes the day?" Perry only brushed past him, snapping "Badly enough!"

Perry knew exactly what had to be done. At once he hoisted his battle flag to signal that he wasn't beaten. The second it unfurled in the wind, loud cheers rang out from the other ships; their crews weren't beaten either. His next order was to tack on every stitch of sail the masts could carry. Lastly, he ordered the carronades loaded with two balls apiece.

Niagara swept forward like an avenging whirlwind. Her commander meant to break the center of the British line, raking the ships on either side as he came through. No one knew it then, but the long battle would be over in another fifteen minutes.

Now came Barclay's turn to worry. The Englishman stared in amazement as the Americans drove headlong toward his flagship. *Niagara*'s first shot snapped some ropes holding *Queen Charlotte*'s topsail in place, making her swerve into *Detroit*. The ships were locked together when Perry passed close by at right angles.

His carronades lived up to their nickname—smashers. Their fiery wind blew a hailstorm of iron across decks crowded with officers and men. The cannonballs were so well-placed that some tore clean through *Queen Charlotte* to smash into *Detroit* alongside. There was a deafening cr-a-a-ck as the flagship's masts came crashing down. *Detroit* was so riddled that one couldn't put a hand on her sides without touching splinters or an imbedded chunk of iron.

Having broken the enemy line, *Niagara*, followed by the gunboats, plowed ahead, raking the enemy vessels from stem to stern. The dazed commanders hauled down their colors without waiting for a second round with the ferocious Yankees.

Perry, too, was dazed. He could hardly believe that he had done the "impossible." One minute he was forced to leave his stricken flagship. The next moment he was master of Lake Erie. Yet there was more. For Perry had chalked up two of history's "firsts": he had fought the United States Navy's first fleet action and, for the only time, caused the Royal Navy to lose an entire squadron.

Perry ended the battle where he had started it — aboard the *Lawrence*. The survivors were silent as he came aboard; they were too exhausted to speak and, besides, their commander didn't need to know what was in their hearts.

Tears welled up in his eyes when he saw the wreckage and the bodies strewn about. A bolt of fear suddenly passed through him. "Where's my brother?" he asked, remembering that Alexander had been left behind. Searchers found the boy asleep in his hammock, worn out from the excitement of the day. He had slept through his brother's victory.

Perry went off to a corner by himself and sat down. His hand reached into his pocket for a pencil stub and an old envelope. He smoothed the crumpled paper and, using a sailor's cap for a desk, wrote a message to General Harrison on the back:

Gen'l.   We have met the enemy and they are ours —
two ships, two brigs, one schooner and one sloop. Yours
with with the greatest esteem and respect,

O. H. Perry.

The sailor's message was the soldier's signal to go into
action. Harrison had been building his army since the spring
of 1813. By early fall he had four thousand five hundred
troops — regulars, Kentucky militia, friendly Indians —
camped along the Ohio shore of Lake Erie. The general
meant to use this army like a huge nutcracker. While the
cavalry under Colonel Richard M. Johnson rode around
the lakeshore to Detroit, Perry's fleet would ferry the rest
of the army to a spot below Fort Malden. The American
forces would then advance, crushing the enemy between
them.

General Proctor read Harrison's mind like an open
book; a two-pronged attack was exactly what he'd have tried
had he been in the American's place. The only thing to do
now that his supply line was cut and the trap about to
close was to escape while there was still time.

Proctor ordered the garrison at Detroit to retreat into
Canada. Preparations were also made to abandon his main
base, Fort Malden, destroying it as he left. The general
would then march eastward to the Niagara frontier, where
his troops were badly needed. American raiders had recently
captured York (present-day Toronto) and burned the Parliament buildings when scalps were found in the main meeting
chamber.

Tecumseh was furious upon learning of the plan. He
had joined the British to fight Americans not to run away.
If his ally gave up Detroit and Fort Malden, the enemy would
regain the entire Northwest Territory, shattering his hopes
for an Indian nation. Tecumseh would rather die fighting
than see such a tragedy fall upon his people.

The Shawnee chief called his followers to a powwow
on the Fort Malden parade ground. As the warriors sat grim-
faced, he went to the "standing stone," a large boulder from
which announcements were made. British officers gathered

nearby, expecting fireworks. Redcoats watched from the nearby barracks.

Tecumseh's voice filled with emotion as he spoke. "I speak in the names of the Indian chiefs and warriors to General Proctor as the representative of the great father, the King. . . . You have arms and ammunition which our great father sent for his red children. If you have an idea of going away, give them to us, and you may go and welcome. Our lives are in the hands of the Great Spirit. He gave to our ancestors the lands which we possess. We are determined to defend them, and if it be His will, our bones will whiten on them, but we will never give them up."

Tecumseh's voice dropped to a whisper, then rose to a thunderclap as he turned to Proctor. He reminded the Briton of his promise to fight to regain the Indians' lands. "But now we see you are pulling back. We are sorry to see that you are getting ready to flee before you ever caught sight of the enemy. We must compare your conduct to a fat animal that carries its tail on its back, but, when frightened, drops it between its legs and runs."

Proctor's face grew pale, then reddened as Tecumseh's words struck like blows. The Indian was calling him a coward to his face and in front of his own officers.

"Listen, father! The Americans have not yet defeated us by land," he continued. "We therefore wish to remain here and fight the enemy if they make an appearance. If they defeat us, we will retreat with you."

Hundreds of braves shouted and sprang to their feet as Tecumseh finished. He had only to give the word and they'd have rushed the British with their tomahawks. Proctor, fearing a massacre, promised to retreat only a few miles to Moraviantown, a village on the Thames River. He chose this spot because the ground was easy to defend with few troops.

The British evacuated Detroit and Fort Malden on September 24, 1813. They got away with little time to spare, for the Americans struck three days later. The people of Detroit heard a distant rumbling that grew louder by the minute. Suddenly a thousand cavalry burst from the woods below the town. Moments later, Colonel Johnson's Kentuckians were being greeted with cheers and tears, hugs and handshakes.

Meanwhile Perry's warships were escorting eighty transports across Lake Erie. Every fife and drum aboard was playing *Yankee Doodle* as the troops jumped onto a pebbly beach three miles below Fort Malden. They met no opposition; indeed, they found the hated "scalp market" abandoned. Its stockade, shipyards, and barracks were still burning as they took possession.

After leaving a thousand infantrymen to guard his supply line, Harrison set out to find the enemy. It was a glorious Canadian autumn. The army marched over leaf-covered roads and forest paths. Maple and oak trees burned golden red in the dazzling sunlight. The cold, clean air refreshed the troops, raising their spirits. Soon they'd have their revenge for the River Raisin massacre.

Proctor had chosen the battleground carefully. The Thames River lay on the left with a high bank that prevented an enemy's coming along the flank, or side, and attacking from behind. Four hundred Redcoats were strung out there in two lines, one behind the other, thirty yards apart. On the right was a small swamp where Tecumseh's braves were posted, their line curving around to a larger swamp. The Indians numbered about one thousand two hundred men. The American force, three thousand five hundred strong, was more than twice the strength of its opponent.

Despite the odds, Tecumseh still hoped for victory. He had been in tight spots before, where courage and skill outweighed mere numbers. They might do so again today.

The Shawnee came up to Proctor to show there were no hard feelings for the past. "Father," he said gently, "have a big heart. Tell your young men to be firm and all will be well." Smiling, he left the general to stroll along the Redcoats' lines and shake their officers' hands. Finally he returned to his own people. To each group he gave the same advice: "Be brave! Stand firm! Shoot straight!" He'd just finished when the metallic notes of a bugle sounded in the distance. The Americans were coming.

Colonel Richard M. Johnson's Kentucky cavalry were to spearhead the assault. These units were unlike any cavalry in the world at this time. Instead of the sword, their basic weapon was the long rifle, a more accurate gun than the army musket. Kentucky riflemen were as expert with the long rifle on horseback as on flat ground — or atop a ship's mast. They also carried pistols, tomahawks, and wicked-looking hunting knives.

"Charge them, my brave Kentuckians," Harrison cried as a bugle sounded. The cavalrymen jabbed spurs into their horses' flanks and bolted forward, shouting "Remember the Raisin!"

Colonel Johnson's brother, James, led his men straight for the Redcoats. The first line crumpled under the shock of horse hoofs and rifle shots. Those who didn't throw up their hands in surrender rushed to join their comrades in the second line.

Their general was also in a hurry — to get away from the scene of action. He had heard the Kentuckians' war cry

The Battle of the River Thames

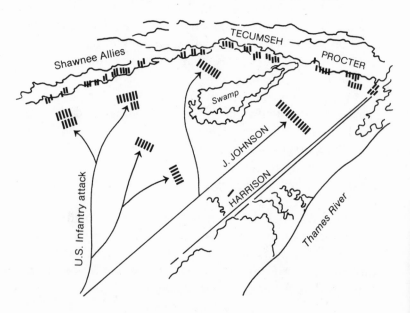

and knew what it meant for him personally. Proctor dashed to a waiting carriage, leaving his troops to buy time for his escape with their lives. But as soon as he turned his back on them, they threw down their muskets and surrendered also. Although Proctor escaped frontier justice, he couldn't avoid the justice of his own army. He was later court-martialed and the court's finding of cowardice read to every unit of the British Army. He never held a command again.

In the meantime Colonel Johnson led his cavalry against the Indians. Tecumseh had no intention of running away. His braves let go a volley of musket fire and charged the oncoming Americans without hesitating.

Once again a bugle sounded, this time signaling the cavalrymen to dismount and advance on foot through the heavy timber. A desperate hand-to-hand struggle broke out in which leaders suffered as much as their men. Colonel Johnson shot a brave who struck him with a tomahawk, then fell unconscious from loss of blood.

Tecumseh was in the thick of the fighting. He ran forward, pausing only to load his musket and fire. "Be brave! Be brave!" he cried, his voice rising above the noise of the battle.

Yet the end was drawing near. Nawkaw, a friend who fought at his side, saw him wounded repeatedly. Blood trickled from his mouth. A red stain on his buckskin shirt showed where a bullet had entered his chest. Still he fought. Still he refused to give up.

All of a sudden fighters on both sides noticed something strange. There were plenty of gunshots and war whoops, but Tecumseh's voice no longer boomed above the battle's sounds. Word of the chief's death spread among his followers like wildfire. Tecumseh had been their guiding spirit and, now that he was gone, they became frightened. They broke and ran.

So ended the Battle of the Thames, October 5, 1813. Victory cost the Americans twenty-five killed and fifty wounded. The British had about thirty-five casualties, plus six hundred taken prisoner. The bodies of thirty-three warriors were counted on the battlefield.

The death of Tecumseh. Although
nobody today knows who killed the
Shawnee chief or how he died, an artist
at the time showed him being shot
by a high-hatted cavalryman.

Tecumseh, however, was not among them. No one today
knows the location of his grave. That night his friends returned to the battlefield and found his body within sight of
the American campfires. They buried him in a secret place,
along with his dream of an American Indian nation.

The men who sat around those campfires wondered if
their old enemy was really dead. No one saw him fall. It
would be just like him to play dead, then spring out of the
darkness like a panther lying in wait. Extra guards were
posted around the camp as a precaution against surprise
attack. And for good measure, the troops slept on their guns,
ready to rise up shooting in an instant.

At midnight the sentries heard a pained, panicked cry: "Indians! O Lord! O Lord! Indians!" In a flash the whole camp sprang to arms. But it was only a false alarm. A Kentucky private, who had seen more than a youngster should in one day, had been having a nightmare.

Harrison broke camp at sunup and headed back to Detroit. Winter was coming and he didn't want to be snowed in so far from home. He had a right to be satisfied with himself. The Northwest Territory was back in American hands and the power of the Indian tribes broken forever. The army had avenged its defeats. Yet peace was further away than ever.

5

Marauders
of the Chesapeake

On May 14, 1814, the ship *Ida* arrived at her home port of Boston. The news she carried sent a shock through the United States Government. Napoleon was defeated. He had been forced to give up his throne as Emperor of the French and leave the country.

Ida's news could only mean that America's war with Great Britain would soon be heating up. For with Napoleon gone, thousands of British regulars became available for service in North America. Time was running out on the War Hawks' plans. If Canada was to be conquered, the job had to be done before midsummer.

A five-thousand-man invasion force was assembled in New York State near Niagara Falls. Their commander was General Jacob Brown, a no-nonsense soldier who knew how to get the best from his men. Brown's second-in-command was Winfield Scott, nicknamed "Old Fuss 'n Feathers" because he loved uniforms dripping with gold braid and hats topped with gorgeous ostrich plumes. Scott's troops, though, wore drab homespun gray, the only cloth available when regulation blue ran out.

Two bloody battles were fought at Chippewa (July 5) and Lundy's Lane (July 25) in which neither side gained a clear victory. We remember Chippewa not as a battle, but because the uniforms of Scott's troops were adopted in their honor as the official uniform of the West Point cadets, who still wear gray. Apart from this, however, the invasion accomplished nothing.

Meanwhile the British high command was making its own plans. Three blows would be aimed at knocking the United States out of the war by year's end. The blows would fall along a north-south line running from New York to the Gulf of Mexico. The first blow, along the shore of Lake Champlain and down the Hudson Valley, would separate New England from the rest of the nation. British forces might even capture New York City, the nation's wealthiest seaport. The second blow would fall in the area of Chesapeake Bay. Since British seapower was unchallenged here, troops could be landed anywhere in hit-and-run raids. Finally, the British would seize New Orleans at the mouth of the Mississippi River. Losing control of the lower Mississippi would block America's westward expansion, squeezing it into a narrow strip along the Atlantic coast.

*   *   *

The British led off with their Chesapeake Bay campaign. Their naval commander was Sir George Cockburn (pronounced "Coburn"). At forty-four, the admiral had served in the Royal Navy since the age of nine. A ship's cabin was the only home he ever knew. He became so used to being at sea that coming ashore made him feel like a stranger on another planet.

Cockburn's fleet sealed the mouth of Chesapeake Bay like a cork in a bottle. Fast-moving units struck the coast at will, brushing aside the local militia as if they were toy soldiers. Cockburn enjoyed playing with the Americans, as cats play with mice. He once sent a seaman to Havre de

Washington during the War of 1812 was still a frontier town carved out of the surrounding wilderness. In this view we see Pennsylvania Avenue and the poplar trees planted by President Jefferson.

Grace, Maryland, with orders to pose as a deserter and say that the British were coming.

"The British are coming!" The alarm spread through the countryside. Churchbells rang. Drums beat. Militia poured into town from far and wide. But when the enemy didn't appear, they scattered, leaving only one sentry to watch the shore.

Cockburn arrived in the sleeping town before dawn next morning. His marines, allowed to loot as they pleased, broke into houses and threw people's possessions into the streets. They roared with laughter when, having torn open feather

beds, the wind scattered the feathers in swirling clouds. When they finished looting and having "fun," they set the town ablaze. Three Maryland towns — Frenchtown, Georgetown, Fredericktown — later suffered the same fate.

The admiral knew that he had a special talent for burning towns. But these places were small fry. He anxiously awaited reinforcements that would enable him to burn a really important place — like Washington, D.C.

Those reinforcements had sailed from Europe at the beginning of June. The five thousand troops crowded aboard the transports were no parade ground showoffs. They wore high leather hats dented and scratched with wear. Their red coats were faded from sweat and sunlight. These were the battle-hardened veterans who had fought the armies of Napoleon for ten years. And their commander, Major General Robert Ross, was sure they'd make mincemeat of the Yankees.

The fleet put into Jamaica after a month at sea to refit and take on supplies. It also took aboard more troops: Negroes, ex-slaves who had joined the British after escaping from Southern plantations. In mid-August, 1814, the fleet dropped anchor in Chesapeake Bay, joining Cockburn's fleet.

The admiral and the general spent hours studying maps of the Washington, D.C., area. They were especially interested in the rivers, natural highways for bringing the war to the gates of the American capital. Washington is built on a peninsula below which the east and west branches of the Potomac River join to flow into Chesapeake Bay. Going upstream, once one passed Alexandria, Virginia, it was clear sailing to the city's back door. Another river, the Patuxent, also empties into the Chesapeake. Although the Patuxent doesn't flow past the capital, it is only forty-five miles from Bladensburg, Maryland, the city's front door. Bladensburg lies on the East Branch of the Potomac. Once across the small wooden bridge there, it was a five-mile walk along a good road to Capitol Hill and the Houses of Congress. Cockburn and Ross meant to knock on Washington's rear and front doors at the same time.

On the morning of August 7, 1814, the British fleet lay off the western shore of Chesapeake Bay. Ships-of-the-line and frigates stood guard as barges filled with Redcoats got underway. One group under Captain James Alexander Gordon sailed up the Potomac. In the days ahead it would loot Alexandria but arrive too late to aid the main force with the capture of Washington.

Cockburn and Ross entered the mouth of the Patuxent with the main force. No attempt was made to hide their movements. Few regular troops were stationed in the area, which meant that the United States capital would be defended by militiamen, no match for the British veterans.

The invaders sailed upstream until they came to Benedict, Maryland, where the troops went ashore. At first the
weather proved more dangerous than the Americans. August
is a miserable month along the Potomac. The temperature
hovers around a hundred degrees; the high temperature and
humidity make it feel like being covered from head to toe
with a woolen blanket soaked with hot water. August is a
time for resting quietly and staying in the shade.

The British could do neither. The air was perfectly still,
not a blade of grass moving as they marched under the
broiling sun. The men raised clouds of dust with their feet,
which flew into their faces. Their eyes and noses ran; dust
crackled between their teeth. In addition to a musket,
bayonet, and eighty cartridges, each Redcoat carried a knapsack filled with extra shirts, stockings, a blanket, food for
three days, and a wooden canteen filled with water. The
knapsack, worn over a woolen coat buttoned to the chin, felt
like a ton of burning coals.

The winding red column did the famous "British quick-
step," alternating three steps running with three steps at a
walk. It was a killing pace even for veterans. Canteens emptied quickly. Men marched with their tongues hanging out of
their mouths. Coming to a stream, they paused only long
enough to swallow a few handfuls of muddy water before
moving on. At least sixty soldiers died of sunstroke, exhaustion, or heart failure.

Late in the morning of the fifth day, August 24, they
arrived at Bladensburg. Peering through the dancing heatwaves, they saw the Americans waiting for them across the
East Branch. Five thousand militia and twenty-five cannon
were drawn up in two lines along a ridge with the Wash-
ington-Bladensburg road passing through the center of their
position.

Ross scanned the enemy through a spyglass, unim-
pressed at their unmilitary appearance. Not only did they
look unsoldierly, they *were* unsoldierly. The American
militia were young, inexperienced, and soft. Few had ever
shot at a person, let alone someone who'd shoot back at them.
War, to nineteen-year-old Private John P. Kennedy and his

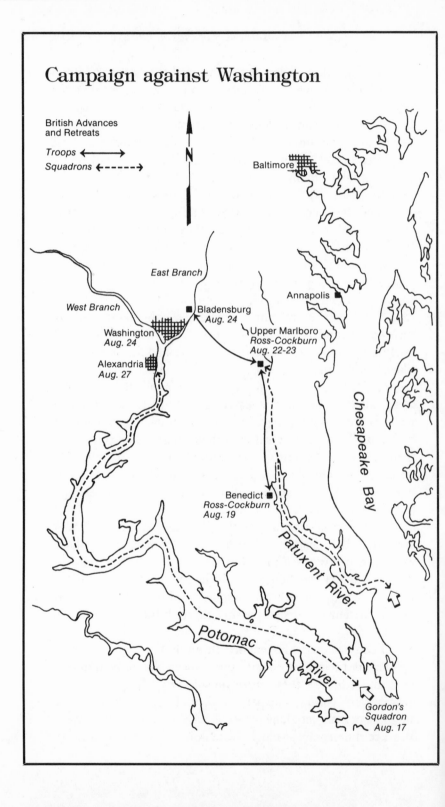

Campaign against Washington

British Advances
and Retreats

Troops ⟵——⟶
Squadrons ⟵- - - ⟶

N

Baltimore

East Branch

West Branch

Annapolis

Bladensburg
Aug. 24

Washington
Aug. 24

Upper Marlboro
*Ross-Cockburn
Aug. 22-23*

Alexandria
Aug. 27

Chesapeake Bay

Benedict
*Ross-Cockburn
Aug. 19*

Patuxent River

Potomac River

Gordon's
*Squadron
Aug. 17*

friends, was a fancy-dress picnic. They traveled in style, with their personal supply wagon filled with cured hams, bread, coffee, and chocolate; a Negro servant named Eliza did all the cooking and cleanup. It was an easy life, and Kennedy was so sure of victory that he brought a pair of dancing slippers to wear at the ball Mrs. Madison would give in the heroes' honor.

General William Henry Winder, the American commander, was less confident. The militia, he felt, were unreliable and would cave in as soon as the Redcoats opened fire. His final orders to Washington's defenders were about the roads they should take when retreating from the battlefield. The battle, in Winder's mind, was lost before it began.

President Madison didn't make the general's job any easier. He had ridden over from Washington to see the battle and give Winder advice — *plenty* of advice. His presence was more bothersome than useful. As the troops waited, the President rode through their lines to see that everything was all right. He became so interested in what he saw that he was about to cross the Bladensburg bridge and ride into the British positions when a soldier warned of the danger. The absent-minded Madison turned back to see the sights from the distance.

The President had just reached safety when Ross ordered the Redcoats to storm the Bladensburg bridge. As they came forward the hillside across the way became dotted with white smoke puffs. The crack of American musketry mingled with the deep roar of artillery. The British column broke and ran back to the safety of the town.

"What will they say in England if we stop now?" said one of Ross's aides as the troops streamed past. Ross, the commander in a dozen battles against Napoleon's finest troops, snapped, "Even if it rains militia, we go on."

The ranks were reformed and sent forward for another try. This time they were helped by a weapon the Americans hadn't seen before: Congreve rockets. The invention of Sir William Congreve, a British artillery officer, these rockets were sheet-iron tubes filled with gunpowder set off by a fuse and launched from copper tubes mounted on wooden

The Congreve Rocket

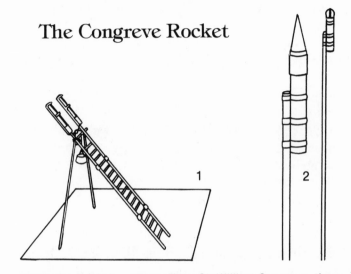

Invented by the English artillery officer Sir William Congreve, these rockets were the first to be used by armies in the Western world. The rocket came in several sizes and shapes, two of which are shown (2), and was fired from a tripod-shaped launching ramp (1).

tripods. Unlike today's missiles, Congreve rockets were impossible to aim with any accuracy, nor could they travel more than a mile. There is no record of them hurting, much less killing, anyone during the War of 1812.

The militia didn't know this at Bladensburg. Winder's men stood wide-eyed as the rockets screeched overhead, trailing streamers of smoke. "Comets! They're shooting comets at us!" someone shouted. The combination of rockets and musketry was too much for the raw troops. Thousands of men dropped their muskets and ran for their lives, crowding the roads leading from the battlefield. Their panicky retreat has been known ever since as "The Bladensburg Races." Madison, seeing the battle lost, galloped away, the only President ever to be with American forces in action.

Had he stayed a little longer he would have seen the Redcoats' advance halted in its tracks. It was halted not by the militia, but by the arrival of five hundred sailors and marines under Joshua Barney. Born in 1759, on a farm near

Baltimore, Barney, as one of fourteen children, had to be self-supporting from an early age. At eleven, he took odd jobs aboard coasters in Chesapeake Bay. By his sixteenth birthday, he was second-in-command of a merchantman, which he brought to port safely after the captain died in a storm. During the Revolution he captained the privateer *Hyder Ally*, in which he captured the British warship *General Monk* in one of the most famous naval actions of the war. It was he who brought home the first news that King George III had recognized American independence.

Barney was fifty-three when the new war with Britain began. He lost no time in applying for privateer's letters and putting to sea in *Rossie*. He later gave up privateering to take a captain's commission in the United States Navy.

Barney was commanding a flotilla, or squadron, of sixteen gunboats on the Patuxent when the British arrived. Since there wasn't a prayer of stopping the enemy with these flimsy one-gun vessels, he put the crews ashore with the ships' guns. As Admiral Cockburn approached, ready for battle, he was amazed to see the line of gunboats explode like a string of firecrackers.

Barney decided that the navy could fight as well as the army on land. Arriving at Washington, he helped himself to ammunition from warehouses at the navy yard despite the guards' protests. His men then put harnesses over their shoulders and pulled five big naval guns toward Bladensburg. This was no easy task, for each gun and its carriage weighed at least two tons.

A large part of Barney's force were tall, muscular Negroes, among them ex-slaves. Brave men, they had proven themselves many times before in battle. When a landlubber asked if they'd run from the Redcoats, Barney roared, "They don't know how to run; they will die at their guns first."

The navy men arrived just as the Bladensburg Races were getting into full swing. Barney immediately set up his guns across the Washington road and waited for the enemy to arrive. Moments later, a solid red column came into view. The temperature was topping the hundred-degree mark, but the Redcoats didn't notice the heat now. Their fighting spirit was aroused and they pressed forward, tasting the excitement of victory.

"We'll give 'em a by-God hot reception," said Barney, turning to Captain Miller of the marines. As he spoke, he slowly raised his right arm and brought it down sharply.

An eighteen-pounder opened fire. The British had never seen such gunnery before on land; a single ball blew a whole company off the road, killing ten and wounding thirty others. Barney squinted, peering into the smoke. "Smite 'em, smite 'em," he kept mumbling to himself.

The British, however, were far from beaten. Regrouping, they waited for reinforcements and advanced through some woods on Barney's right. This time they charged with fixed bayonets, while rockets whooshed overhead.

Barney's seadogs held their ground; it took more than noise to frighten men used to standing up to cannon balls and flying splinters. The sailors, armed with pistols and swords, shouted "Board 'em! Board 'em!" and charged. The marines let out a bloodcurdling yell and advanced with fixed bayonets. Again the enemy retreated.

General Ross decided to waste no more lives on frontal assaults. Barney's force was small and therefore easy to surround. While Redcoats moved in from right and left, the Fourth (King's Own) Regiment went on a wider encircling movement. Soon the American gunners were falling by twos and threes. But as fast as they fell, others took their place. Yet when Barney himself went down with a bullet in the hip, they knew the battle was ending. The captain lay beside a cannon, grinding his teeth in pain. "Get away," he ordered the survivors. "I'll stay where I've fallen. I'm not afraid of the Redcoats."

Ross and Cockburn were walking up the hill to inspect the Yankee position when they noticed the dead were wearing naval uniforms. "I told you it was the flotilla men!" said the admiral with pride. Ross nodded in agreement. "Yes," he replied, "they have given us our only real fighting."

The British commanders found Barney beside his cannon. They came up, introduced themselves, and congratulated him warmly on the fight he'd given them.

Barney's wounds were treated and he was made a prisoner of war. Although Barney's battle was over, his countrymen's ordeal was only beginning. As soon as camp was made for the wounded at Bladensburg, the Redcoats set out again. Ahead lay an open road leading to a defenseless city.

* * *

That city was nothing like the magnificent capital we know today. Washington, D.C., in 1814 was in many ways still a settlement hacked out of the wilderness between Virginia and Maryland. Although the government had moved into its quarters fourteen years earlier, axemen could still be seen chopping down trees to make way for the streets. A hunter needn't have been bored in old Washington, not when grouse, deer, even wolves, could be shot within the city limits.

Life was often unpleasant for the eight thousand Washingtonians, half of whom were Negro slaves or freedmen. The city had no police, which made going about town risky. Since there were only three street lamps in the whole city, and since these were usually broken, it was best to stay indoors after dark. When it rained, the cellars flooded and the streets filled knee-deep with mud. During the dry season, swirling dust got into everything, including the cooking pots.

Then, as now, Congress met in the United States Capitol built atop Capitol Hill in the eastern part of the city. In President Madison's time the Capitol consisted of two limestone buildings — one for the House of Representatives, the other for the Senate — connected by a wooden passageway. The great dome crowned with the statue of Freedom wasn't put in place until President Lincoln's time. During rainstorms puddles collected under the capitol's skylights. The lawmakers were sometimes interrupted by gunshots as hunters stalked gamebirds in the surrounding fields.

Pennsylvania Avenue was a wide, unpaved road that ran west for a mile and a half from Capitol Hill. The city's main street, it passed the President's House, also known as the President's Palace. The president's home was built near an undrained swamp, so that the First Family was serenaded by the cawing of crows by day and the croaking of frogs by night. Nobody got used to the buzzing of mosquitoes, which rose in clouds from marshes along the Potomac.

Although begun in 1792, President's House was not completed for many years. Only a flimsy rail fence separated it from its nearest neighbor, a racetrack. Townspeople could wander the grounds at will; the president had no bodyguards, only a butler and some servants, among them Negro slaves.

Only six rooms were usable when John and Abigail Adams moved in in 1800; there were no indoor toilets. Mrs. Adams used to hang the family laundry, washed by herself, in a large unfinished room that would later be the famous

East Room. President Jefferson, the house's second tenant, built bathrooms and had two wells dug to provide fresh water, which otherwise had to be carried in buckets from five blocks away. President Madison and his wife, Dolley, bought fine furniture and decorations for the public rooms and private apartments on the second floor. The Madisons also had the building painted white. From then on the president's home has been called the White House.

Dolley Madison was a charming, easygoing person who, some said, was the most beautiful woman in town. At least once a week she visited the markets with her slave, Sukey.

The President's House, later called the White House, as it appeared about the beginning of the War of 1812. Stonecutters in the lower left of the picture are working on limestone blocks to complete the building.

The women carried baskets and spent hours bargaining for provisions to keep the White House kitchen well-stocked. People enjoyed meeting her and listening to her just-plain-folks talk.

The First Lady had no time for small talk on August 24, 1814. She was worried about her husband, who had ridden to Bladensburg early that morning. She'd run back and forth to a top-floor window every few minutes to train her spyglass in the direction of the battlefield. She could see the shimmering heatwaves and hear the muffled rumbling of artillery. When away from her observation post, she packed. Government papers, books, silverware and other valuables were crammed into trunks which servants loaded into a carriage at the front door. "Mr. Madison comes not; may God protect him!" she scribbled in a note to her sister at three o'clock. Moments later a dustcovered messenger galloped up the driveway, waving his hat and shouting, "Clear out! Clear out!" The British were coming and she had to escape from the doomed capital.

The First Lady, however, wasn't ready to clear out right way. Colonel Charles Carroll, a family friend, had come by to encourage her to leave. "The British will be here at any moment," he said. "Ma'am, you must leave at once."

"Yes, Colonel," she replied, cool as a cucumber, "as soon as I get this picture down."

"Picture! Picture!" Carroll exploded. "Ma'am, I beg you. There is not time to bother with a picture."

Oh, yes, there was — with *this* picture. A life-size portrait of George Washington by Gilbert Stuart hung on the dining room wall. The enemy, she knew, would enjoy insulting this image of the nation's first president. And the wife of its fourth president meant to deprive them of that bit of entertainment at least.

The painting, which hangs in the White House today, was in a heavy frame screwed to the wall. Mrs. Madison had the gardener chop the frame apart with a hatchet and remove the canvas. On the way out, she snatched up a copy of the Declaration of Independence bearing the signatures of the founding fathers. "They shan't have this either," she in-

President Madison's wife, Dolley, refused to leave the doomed capital until she rescued a portrait of George Washington and a copy of the Declaration of Independence.

sisted. "The British would be pleased to burn this precious document." Indeed, they'd have liked nothing better.

Escaping from the capital took courage and luck. Panicky people raced through the streets, expecting the worst if the enemy caught them. A mob of hoodlums formed on the White House grounds to curse the president. "Go find your husband for us so we can hang him," someone shouted. Mrs. Madison turned pale. "Hang Madison!" shouted another. Colonel Carroll drew two pistols and glared at the crowd, which parted, allowing the overloaded carriage to pass.

The Redcoats arrived toward nightfall. A pale moon lit their way down Maryland Avenue toward the Capitol, a dark, massive shape outlined against the sky. The soldiers were tense, as though entering a ghost town. Deserted streets, houses shuttered and silent, greeted them. Drummers beat a long roll, the signal for the city's leaders to come for a formal

Buildings blaze as General Ross' infantry march into downtown Washington. The sailors in the lower right part of the picture are tearing down a building for firewood.

surrender ceremony. The drum rolls echoed down the streets, fading away into the distance. Fifteen minutes later, the Redcoats stood in ranks before the Capitol. Like the other buildings, it was silent and darkened; padlocks and chains held the huge doors shut.

Ross and Cockburn knew what would come next. Their orders were clear: burn all United States Government property in reprisal for the raid on York. Private property should be spared so long as homeowners cooperated and had no weapons. The moment weapons were found in a house, it would be burned. Any citizen caught with weapons in hand would be shot.

The general took no chances with snipers. At his signal the first ranks fired a volley through the Capitol's windows. The crack of musketry was answered by the sound of breaking glass and lead balls glancing off the walls inside. An assault company then raced up the stairs at double time to shoot off the padlocks. The invaders streamed through the open doors into the home of the United States Congress. It was the grimmest moment in all the nation's history.

Cockburn led his men into the House of Representatives. Mounting the rostrum, he sprawled in the speaker's chair, looking every inch an old pirate chief holding court.

"Now hear this!" he bellowed. "Shall this harbor of Yankee democracy be burned? All in favor say Aye."

"Aye! Aye! Aye! Aye!" the sailors chanted. Grinning, their admiral ruled that the ayes had won the vote — democratically. And now to work.

Axe-swinging sailors and soldiers ran through the House and Senate chambers, chopping up the seats of the galleries and tossing them to the floor below. Desks, chairs, tables, books, and official papers were heaped in the center of the floor of each chamber. Barrels of gunpowder were emptied over the kindling and ignited with Congreve rockets.

The United States Capitol burst into flame, together with the Supreme Court and Library of Congress, which used to share the building. Sheets of flame leaped from doorways and windows. Windblown sparks gushed from the roof in great swirls.

The blazing Capitol dominated the night sky. James Madison, riding over the Virginia countryside to rejoin his wife, turned in the saddle to see the distant flames. Far down the Potomac, the captain of a British warship noted the fire in his logbook. In Baltimore, forty miles to the northeast, people stood on the rooftops to see the glowing horizon.

The Redcoats, meanwhile, turned their backs on the flames and marched down Pennsylvania Avenue toward the White House. An inn owned by Mrs. Barbara Suter stood across the street. Ross knocked on the door to announce that British officers would be joining her for dinner in a little while. She knew what *that* meant and was frightened.

The invaders found the White House as Dolley Madison had left it. Upstairs, the president's clothes lay helter-skelter on beds or stuffed into half-filled traveling bags. An officer, who hadn't been out of his clothes for a week, noticed the finest, whitest underwear he'd ever seen. Stripping off his uniform, he exchanged his evil-smelling underwear for Mr. Madison's spotless linens.

Soldiers were amazed to find the dining room table set for forty guests. The president had left instructions for the servants to prepare a dinner that he, Dolley, and the cabinet would enjoy after the victory at Bladensburg. Wines were chilling in ice-filled coolers. Cold cuts were set out in trays in the pantry. The British enjoyed the president's meal, then turned his house into a bonfire in appreciation.

The firemaking so pleased Admiral Cockburn that he rode a mule through Mrs. Suter's front door and into her dining room. He trotted up to the table and, blowing out the candles, said he'd eat by the light of the building burning across the street. General Ross, a more serious man, went on with his meal without looking up. Satisfied at last, the officers rejoined the troops for the march back to camp on Capitol Hill, where they spent the night.

Few people, soldiers or civilians, slept well that night. As the worried citizens wondered about what tomorrow would bring, a thunderstorm pelted the city, turning the British camp into a muddy mess. But at least it drowned the fires, ending the danger that the flames might spread to the

The burning of Washington as seen from the Potomac River.

whole city. Although the Capitol was gutted, its walls remained intact. Scorch marks can be seen in places to this day. The walls of the White House also remained standing, even though the roof collapsed. It, too, would be rebuilt.

The Redcoats returned to their work next morning, August 25. The United States Treasury, Post Office Department, War Department, and State Department were set afire. The navy yard had already been burned by its own commander rather than have its war materials fall into enemy hands. Cockburn's sailors had to be satisfied with destroying the few buildings that had escaped the flames the night before. When they saw that nothing remained to be burned,

The White House after the fire of 1814. Although the British succeeded in destroying the building's interior, the stout walls remained intact, making it possible to rebuild the president's home.

the British evacuated the city. After picking up their wounded at Bladensburg, the army retraced its steps to Benedict, where it met the transports.

The destruction of Washington was the high-water mark of the British effort to knock the United States out of the war. At a cost of about a thousand men — two hundred killed, four hundred wounded, four hundred dead of exhaustion, captured, or deserted — they had humiliated the young nation.* Yet, had they been able to see into the future, the British commanders might not have been so pleased with their success.

The fires of Washington did what President Madison had been unable to do: fire American patriotism and unite most of the country behind the war effort. Even the war's opponents now closed ranks against the "British barbarians." After Washington, the Americans would never suffer a serious defeat, the enemy never enjoy a major victory.

*   *   *

The campaign to cut New England off from the rest of the country got underway a few days after Ross's troops clambered out of their transports. Sir George Prevost, Governor General of Canada, advanced on Lake Champlain with eleven thousand veterans recently arrived from Europe. British spirits were high, for victory seemed certain. Opposing them on land were thirty-three hundred Americans, regulars and militiamen, under General Alexander Macomb. On the lake their sixteen warships faced an equal number of American craft under Captain Thomas Macdonough.

On Sunday, September 11, 1814, Prevost launched a combined ground and naval assault on Plattsburg, New York, at the head of Lake Champlain. Once in his hands, he intended to use the town to anchor his drive southward. Because the roads were so poor, the British needed the Lake Champlain–Hudson River waterways to bring supplies to their troops ashore.

Prevost, however, hadn't reckoned with the American commanders. General Macomb turned out to be another William Henry Harrison, Captain Macdonough another Oliver Hazard Perry. While Macomb's infantry fought the Redcoats to a standstill outside Plattsburg, Macdonough whipped their naval comrades in a two-hour slugging match on the lake. A British naval officer who had fought at

---

* American losses were much smaller: about forty killed, sixty wounded, and one hundred and twenty captured, nearly all at Bladensburg.

Onlookers ashore watch Thomas MacDonough defeat the British at the Battle of Lake Champlain in New York State.

Trafalgar said that that was "child's play" compared to Lake Champlain. The American victory ended the danger of invasion from the North. Prevost retreated to Canada, where his forces remained until the war's end.

*   *   *

On that very day, lookouts on rooftops in Baltimore sighted the tall masts of warships approaching through Chesapeake Bay. The vessels came on boldly under clouds of canvas that glistened in the morning sun. Cockburn and Ross had joined

forces with Vice Admiral Sir Alexander Cochrane's squadron. The combined fleet, fifty ships strong and under Cochrane's overall command, was coming to take Baltimore.

Baltimore's forty-five thousand people had been expecting them for a long time. The British, they knew, hated their city more than any other in the United States. The nation's third largest, Baltimore had grown wealthy through shipbuilding and privateering. No privateers boasted a better record — over five hundred British merchantmen taken or sunk. His Majesty's Government would be very generous to

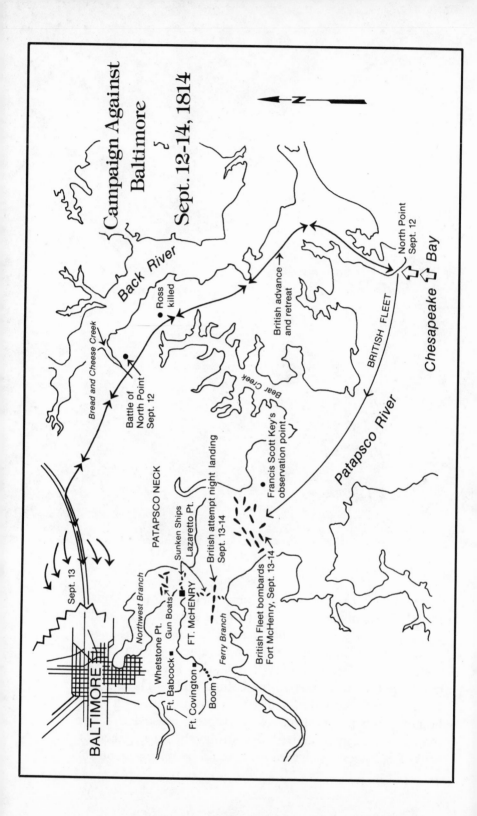

Campaign Against Baltimore
Sept. 12-14, 1814

N

Chesapeake Bay

North Point
Sept. 12

BRITISH FLEET

Patapsco River

Back River

Ross killed

Bread and Cheese Creek

Battle of North Point
Sept. 12

British advance and retreat

Bear Creek

Francis Scott Key's observation point

British attempt night landing
Sept. 13-14

British Fleet bombards
Fort McHenry, Sept. 13-14

PATAPSCO NECK

Sunken Ships

Lazaretto Pt.

Northwest Branch

Whetstone Pt.

Gun Boats

Ft. Babcock

FT. McHENRY

Ft. Covington

Ferry Branch

Boom

BALTIMORE

Sept. 13

the commanders who settled scores with this "den of Yankee piracy."

Baltimore lies between the forks of the Patapsco River, another of the streams emptying into Chesapeake Bay. The Patapsco's Northwest Branch passes through the very heart of the city, while the Ferry Branch comes within a mile of it. Fort McHenry stands at the tip of the peninsula where the forks join, guarding the narrow channel to the inner harbor.

Although Baltimore's defenses were strengthened early in the war, the burning of Washington spurred its citizens to a supreme effort. The whole population was drafted into the city's defense. Committees formed in each district to care for the wounded; women's groups gathered to tear bed-sheets into strips and roll them into bandages. Children acted as messengers.

Every able-bodied man not needed for military service was sent to the hills at the city's eastern approaches to build fortifications. Thousands turned out each day, rain or shine, to dig trenches and throw up breastworks, chest-high walls of earth. "White and black are at work together," a young lady wrote to her brother in New York. "You'll see a master and his slave digging side by side. There is no distinction whatsoever."

Baltimore became an armed camp. Sailors whose ships were blockaded in ports along the coast arrived in wagon-loads under the familiar flag "Free Trade and Sailors' Rights." Among them were Joshua Barney's heroes of Bladensburg. Militia units poured in from Maryland, Virginia, and Pennsylvania. Regular Army troops took up positions at key points around the city. Altogether, over ten thousand men and one hundred cannon stood ready to repel an invasion.

Their commander was sixty-two-year-old General Samuel Smith, a hardboiled veteran of the Revolution. Sam, as everyone called him, rattled off orders nonstop for a week after taking command. Seeing a weak point in the harbor defenses, he had two dozen ships sunk in line across the Northwest and Ferry Branches to block the city's water approaches. Two small forts were also hastily built and their guns trained to sweep the harbor in a crossfire.

Baltimore's people were in church when the invasion fleet came into view. Cannon shots rang out, calling the defenders to their units. Men jumped to their feet, kissed their families goodbye, and ran home for their muskets. Ministers closed their Bibles or interrupted their sermons in mid-sentence. Reverend John Gruber sent his congregation on its way with a blessing and a prayer—for the enemy. "May the Lord bless King George, convert him, and take him to heaven, as we want no more of him."

Horsemen kept watch on the fleet's movements during the rest of the day and through the night. At dawn, September 12, they saw the ships drop anchor off North Point at the mouth of the Patapsco about fourteen miles from the city. Even at a distance of several miles, they could see rows of red figures standing in barges as oars rose and dipped into the water. Within two hours Ross and Cockburn were ashore with forty-seven-hundred Redcoats, sailors, marines, and rocketmen.

The British commanders rode at the head of the column at a leisurely pace. Unlike the Washington campaign, the weather now was comfortable and their spirits high. After covering half the distance to the city, they stopped at a farm for lunch about noon. Ross had remounted and was ready to leave when the farmer asked if he'd be back for supper. "No," the general replied, a broad smile on his face. "I'll eat in Baltimore tonight — or in hell."

The smile soon left his face. As the column moved along the road, its advance guard ran into a wall of gunfire. Sam Smith had sent out fourteen-hundred troops under General John Stricker to delay the British while he made sure Baltimore's main defenses were in order.

Ross, hearing the shooting, was rushing to the scene of action when snipers shot him from the saddle. The Redcoats knew something was wrong when they saw his riderless horse galloping along the column with streaks of blood on its sides. Moments later, they passed the general stretched out on a blanket at the roadside. A groan passed from rank to rank as they realized that their general was dead. Ross's body was carried to the flagship, where sailors crammed it into a rum barrel to preserve it until it could be sent to his wife for burial.

The Redcoats were out for revenge and didn't hesitate when Colonel Arthur Brook, Ross's second-in-command, ordered a charge. Although outnumbering the Americans four to one, they quickly realized that this was no repeat of the Bladensburg Races. As at Bladensburg, some militiamen ran away when rockets streaked overhead, but the rest stood their ground. After a two-hour firefight, General Stricker withdrew in good order. The Redcoats were too exhausted to pursue and made camp for the night on the battlefield.

The British had another taste of Yankee hospitality next morning, September 13. Upon reaching Baltimore's eastern defenses, they saw the sun reflecting off thousands of bayonets. Colonel Brooke realized at once that it would be suicidal to go further without a diversion, something to make the Americans lower their guard. He needed the navy to sail into Baltimore harbor and land troops in the enemy's rear.

Yet nothing could enter the harbor until Fort McHenry was taken or destroyed. This star-shaped fort of red brick and stone mounted a battery of fifty-seven guns and had furnaces for heating cannon balls. Its thousand-man garrison was commanded by Major George Armistead, an experienced artillery officer. You'd never mistake Armistead's command for anything other than an American post. The major was so proud of his assignment that he flew the granddaddy of American flags over its battlements. The forty-two by thirty-foot flag, which may be seen today in Washington's Smithsonian Institution, had eight red and seven white stripes, plus fifteen stars, one for each state in the union.

Armistead's flag was flapping in the light breeze when the British ships took up their positions. These were not ordinary warships, which would have run aground in the shallows near the fort, but special bombardment vessels. They bore fearsome names like *Devastation, Terror, Meteor,*

British Bomb Ship

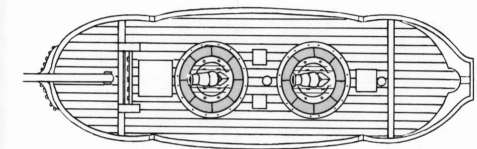

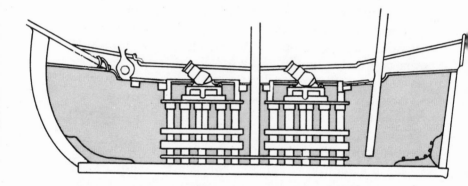

Mortars were very heavy weapons, making it necessary to build special supports under them to prevent them from falling through the bottom of the vessel or shaking it apart when fired.

and *Volcano*. One, the *Erebus*, the ancient Greek name for hell, had dozens of metal tubes for launching Congreve rockets. The others were "bomb ships" carrying mortars, short-barreled cannon for throwing shells, called bombs, at high angles. British bombs were hollow iron balls packed with gunpowder; a fuse, ignited as the bomb left the mortar, set off the explosive charge when it reached its target. Each mortar could hurl a bomb two-and-a-half miles.

The bomb ships stood just beyond range of Fort McHenry's batteries and blasted away at will. Hundreds of bombs and rockets rained down upon the fort, whose defenders could only dive for cover as explosions shook the ground. Fountains of earth shot skyward. Chunks of masonry whizzed through the air. Men's teeth rattled; their ears rang.

Yet Armistead's men led charmed lives — most of them. One bomb crashed through the roof of a magazine filled with barrels of gunpowder. The black sphere spun around the floor, its fuse sputtering until a quick-thinking soldier doused it with a bucket of water. Another bomb exploded above a gun, killing its crew. These, plus twenty-four wounded, were the only American casualties during the bombardment. People called it a miracle.

Eight miles down the Patapsco, a tiny American vessel, the *Minden*, bobbed amid the empty British transports. A thirty-three-year-old Virginia lawyer named Francis Scott Key paced the deck nervously. Little did he suspect when he began his mission that he'd be a bystander at a great battle.

The British had arrested his friend, Dr. William Beanes, for capturing stragglers when their army left Washington. Learning of the arrest, Key went to President Madison for permission to visit the enemy fleet to negotiate his friend's release. Madison agreed with the plan and allowed Key to use the *Minden* as a flag-of-truce ship.

Before leaving, Key and his traveling companion, Colonel John Skinner, asked some British prisoners if they'd like to send letters to friends in the fleet. Did they! In one letter, a sergeant wrote enthusiastically about the care Americans gave wounded prisoners and how grateful he was for their kindness.

Key was welcomed aboard the British flagship and invited to dinner with the commanders. Things went well until he spoke of his mission. The doctor, said Ross, flushing with anger, deserved a rope, not freedom. Without saying another word, Key handed over the sergeant's letter. After reading it, the general agreed that one kindness deserved another. The doctor could go — later. But since the attack on Baltimore was about to begin, the Americans would have to remain under guard aboard *Minden* to keep them from telling about what they'd seen.

Thus Key, Beanes, and Skinner had a ringside seat at

View of the British bombardment of Fort McHenry in Baltimore Harbor. Francis Scott Key watched the warships hurl their bombs high into the air, then saw them crash into the fort.

the bombardment of Fort McHenry. As patriots, they knew that Baltimore's loss would be a crushing blow for the nation. Everything depended upon the fort's holding out. And as long as Armistead's flag flew above its walls, they knew all was well.

The flag continued to fly proudly during the daylight bombardment, except when drifting smoke hid it from time to time.

As nighttime came the flag faded from sight. The bombardment now was at once terrible and beautiful. Rockets slashed across the sky, glaring red against the smoke. Bombs streaked upward in graceful arcs, then, reaching their peak, plunged earthward trailing banners of flame. Some burst in midair, showering the fort with white-hot fragments of iron.

The three Americans looked at each other anxiously, wondering if the flag was still flying over the fort. During that whole miserable night they caught only glimpses of it in the flash and crash of explosions. Only when the first light of dawn revealed the flag in all its glory did they know for sure that Americans still held Fort McHenry. Better still, they learned that the British had given up trying to take the city. Warships were already weighing anchor for the long journey to Halifax.

Key was so moved by his experience that he began to sketch some lines of poetry on the back of a letter. "Oh say can you see, by the dawn's early light. . . . The land of the free and the home of the brave."

Released at last, Scott worked on the poem in the rowboat that took him ashore. Next morning, Tuesday, September 15, 1814, he brought the finished work to a printer's shop. By afternoon, copies of "The Defense of Fort McHenry" were circulating in Baltimore and the outlying communities. Soon the entire country knew of the poem. The verses were not only recited but sung to the tune of "To Anacreon in Heaven," a popular English tavern song. We know it as "The Star-Spangled Banner."

6

Old Hickory

The British might have won the war despite their defeats at Lake Champlain and Baltimore. That they failed, however, is due to the skill and determination of an unusual man. ·

He stood six-feet-one-inch in his stockings. Narrow shoulders, spindly legs, and a rail-thin body made him look like the victim of some horrible wasting sickness. Far from handsome, his long pale face was pitted with smallpox scars and a longer, whitened scar that ran from the left cheek to the forehead. Harsh steel-blue eyes seemed to go through people like icy daggers. He was polite to ladies, but spat around menfolk. His name was Andrew Jackson, and one day he'd be the seventh president of the United States.

His parents, Andrew and Elizabeth Jackson, had come to America from Northern Ireland with their young sons, Hugh and Robert. Traveling overland from the coast, they settled in the Waxhaws, a farming district on the border between North and South Carolina. Mr. Jackson spent months in backbreaking toil to clear the land, until it killed him with overwork. Two weeks later, March 15, 1767, his wife gave birth to their third son, naming him for the father he'd never known.

The future president's early life was hard, but no harder than any youngster's growing up on the frontier. He did his share of the farm chores and attended a one-room school-house whenever he pleased, which wasn't often. Unlike Abraham Lincoln, our other frontier-bred president, Jackson was no scholar. He preferred running around with his friends to burying his nose in books. Inattention to studies explains why Jackson was our worst-educated president. Throughout his life he knew little of history, geography, science, or the classics of literature. His spelling was one of the wonders of the world. Even during his years in the White House, he might spell a word three different ways on the same page. It is said that "O.K.," that most popular American expression, came from his habit of scrawling "Oll Korrect" on papers that met his approval.

Widow Jackson's family sided with the patriots during the American Revolution. When her oldest son, Hugh, died in the war at sixteen, his brothers took his place. Andrew was only thirteen when he joined in skirmishes against Tories, Americans loyal to the King, and British cavalry patrols.

The Jackson brothers once hid in a relative's house after Redcoats broke up an ambush. But a Tory neighbor had seen them and the boys were arrested next morning as they sat at the breakfast table. The British cavalry commander, an arrogant, loudmouthed lieutenant, demanded that Andy clean his boots. The youngster refused, insisting that he be treated as a war prisoner. Knowing him, his refusal was probably neither softspoken or polite. Whereupon the officer raised his sword and brought it down with all his might. The blow might have beheaded Jackson had he not raised his arm to push it aside. In any case, his left hand was cut to the bone and a deep gash opened on his forehead. Those scars would cost the British plenty in years to come.

The Jackson brothers were then marched forty miles without food or water to a prison camp at Camden, South Carolina. The place was without medicines, beds, or blankets

Andrew Jackson was a frontier fighter, lawyer, judge, and general who went on to become the seventh President of the United States.

for the prisoners. Smallpox raged through the camp, and it wasn't long before the boys came down with the disease. Although their mother persuaded the camp commander to release her sons because of their age, Robert died on the way home.

Andy was recovering slowly when Mrs. Jackson decided to care for Waxhaw men in other British prisons. During one of her visits she was struck down by a mysterious disease called "ship fever." Andy never had a chance to say goodbye to his mother, although she said goodbye to him in her own way.

Before she died, Mrs. Jackson wrote Andy a long letter. The letter tells not only of a mother's love for a son far away, but is filled with wisdom about life and getting along with others. Be honest, she wrote, and never forget another's kindness. Above all, she wanted him to be "a true man," to respect himself and stand up for his rights. "Never wound the feelings of others. Never brook wanton outrage upon your own feelings."

Andy took her advice to heart and was guided by it always. Yet he could never bring himself to follow one other piece of advice: "If ever you have to vindicate your feelings or defend your honor do it calmly. If angry at first, wait until your wrath cools off before you proceed." Andy grew from being an angry boy into a hard, sour-faced man with a hair-trigger temper. He seldom smiled and had no sense of humor, least of all about himself.

Once, as a teenager, some friends gave him a musket into which they had loaded a double charge of gunpowder. When he pulled the trigger, the kickback knocked him into the mud. The boys' laughter was cut short when Andy rose to his feet, fists balled, shouting that he'd kill the next one who laughed. They backed off, for everyone knew that he could fight; indeed, he *liked* to fight. Savage brawls were common among frontiersmen. There was no such thing as fighting "cleanly"; you did anything to beat an opponent, including eye-gouging, nose-biting, tongue-pulling, kicking, and stabbing. And Andy Jackson was master of all these tactics. Smart people spoke softly to him and kept a respectful distance.

The Revolution over, he moved to the village of Salisbury in the North Carolina backwoods, where he "read" law. Since there were no law schools then, someone who wanted to become a lawyer lived in the home of an established attorney who helped him prepare for the bar examination. The test couldn't have been difficult, for Jackson passed, even though he spent more time fighting and gambling than studying.

After two years, he felt the urge to wander once more. Crossing the Appalachian Mountains, he made for a jumble of log cabins in Tennessee called Nashville, where he hung up his lawyer's shingle. It was there that he met and married Rachel Donelson Robards. The couple had no children of their own, but adopted an infant boy, christened Andrew Jackson, Junior.

Here, too, Jackson killed his first man face to face. His hot temper boiled over when a fellow named Charles Dickinson passed a cruel remark about Rachel. Jackson challenged him to a duel and shot him dead. There was nothing unusual about such behavior. Dueling was a carryover from the Middle Ages, when gentlemen were supposed to defend their "honor" with sword or pistol. Jackson fought a dozen duels in his lifetime, but Dickinson was the only opponent who died.

Tennessee was the Wild West of the 1790s. Lying hundreds of miles beyond the settled frontier, it was a place where the young and venturesome might rise quickly in the world. Jackson rose — high and fast. His prosperous law practice allowed him to buy the Hermitage, a large estate with a big house, and become a slaveowner. Negro slavery was widespread in the South and Jackson didn't see anything wrong with owning other people.

Jackson entered politics, becoming Tennessee's first Representative in Congress; he also served a term in the United States Senate. Congress, however, seemed too tame and he returned to Nashville to become a judge of the Tennessee Supreme Court. Judge Jackson was just, fearless, and honest. No one acted up in his courtroom, for he kept two loaded pistols on his desk and didn't hesitate to point them at unruly persons. He believed courts and laws existed to do justice, nothing more, nothing less. "Do what is right between these parties," he'd tell juries. "That is what the law always means."

Judges are people of words and papers, while Jackson at thirty-eight was still a man of action. Resigning his judgeship in 1802, he was elected major general in command of the Tennessee militia. Although he'd never led troops in battle or studied military science, he felt that he had a natural ability for warfare. What he didn't already know about soldiering he'd learn on the job. And so Jackson spent the next decade as a country gentleman and part-time general. Few people knew him outside his home state until the War of 1812 made him famous overnight.

*   *   *

As soon as the war began, the War Department asked Tennessee's governor for militia units to drive the British out of Florida. Florida at this time belonged to Spain, Britain's ally in the Napoleonic Wars. Although neutral in the American struggle, Spain went out of its way to be "neutral" in favor of Britain. The Royal Navy freely used Florida's harbors, especially Pensacola, as if they were home ports.

Jackson, as militia commander, was chosen to lead the Florida expedition. During the winter of 1812–1813, he gathered two thousand troops from all over Tennessee. While the cavalry marched overland, the main force boarded flatboats and floated down the Cumberland, Ohio, and Mississippi Rivers. Arriving at Natchez, they learned the meaning of one of the oldest Army expressions: "Hurry up and wait."

They were on a dangerous winter mission and now had to wait for further orders from Washington. They waited. And waited some more. Weeks passed until word finally came that the invasion was cancelled. Jackson was to dismiss the troops and let them make their way home as best they could.

He'd do no such thing! Those boys trusted him; he knew many of them personally or had business dealings with their folks. To leave them flat eight hundred miles from home without pay or food or medicine would be shameful. Digging deep into his pockets, the general used his own money to buy wagons and supplies; he even wrote to Nashville to borrow more money on his personal credit.

Even so, it was rough going crosscountry in midwinter. Bridges had to be built over streams and trails hacked through the woods. Jackson was everywhere, seeing to everything. A bundle of nervous energy, he went days without sleep, seemingly tireless. "He's tough as hickory," a soldier remarked after he passed by. "He's tough as *old* hickory," another chimed in. Hickory was the hardest living thing these frontiersmen knew. And Jackson was like that wood: tough, dependable, and, to them, handsome. The name Old Hickory followed him from then on. He had proven himself a "real man." These frontier roughnecks would follow him anywhere next time. They loved him.

Back at the Hermitage, Old Hickory bombarded the War Department with requests for another assignment. While waiting for a reply, he got into a tavern brawl with Thomas Hart Benton, the future senator from Missouri, and his brother, Jesse. The Bentons shot him in the left shoulder and would have killed him if John Coffee, a huge bear of a man and one of Jackson's close friends, hadn't stepped in at the last moment.

Old Hickory was alive, but only barely. Blood gushed from his shoulder, soaking through two thick mattresses. Every doctor in town came to his room at the Nashville Inn to try his skill. Nothing helped. The bleeding continued and Jackson grew weaker by the day. The doctors grew so desperate that they suggested amputating the arm to save his life. "I'll keep my arm," the general growled, and continued bleeding. At last the bleeding stopped almost completely on its own.

Jackson was lying in bed, feverish and weak, when a messenger brought word that the Creek Indians were on the warpath. The Creeks, a powerful tribe that lived in present-day Alabama and Mississippi, had lived peacefully with the whites until Tecumseh's visit in the fall of 1812. The Shawnee chief told them that peace was only temporary, lasting only so long as the Americans didn't need their lands. The Indians, he said, had a true friend in the British. Already they had captured Detroit and would go on to push the Americans back to the coast. Now was the time to act. If the Creeks revolted, the Great Father across the sea would send all the guns they needed. The Creeks voted for war and, true to Tecumseh's promise, British agents at Pensacola began sending guns upcountry.

The result became clear on August 29, 1813, at Fort Mims in the Mississippi Territory, near the Florida border. It was a blistering hot day and the settlers who crowded into the fort lazed about in the shade. The guards also took

Creek Indians stormed the open gate at Fort Mims and killed all but seventeen of the settlers and soldiers.

it easy beside the gate, which stood wide open. Suddenly the Creeks burst from cover and stormed the entrance. Of the 553 people in Fort Mims, only seventeen were captured and enslaved by the Indians. The rest — men, women, children — were massacred.

Although Tennesseeans weren't involved, as frontier people they had a deep fear of Indians. They could remember a time, not long ago, when Indians killed at least one settler a week on the outskirts of Nashville. The Creek uprising had to be crushed, and Andrew Jackson was the best man for the job.

The thought of action was a tonic to the ailing man. "The health of your general is restored," he wrote from his sickbed, a pillow for his desk. "I will lead in person." Groggy and pale, his shoulder bound so tightly that only a little blood seeped through the bandage, Old Hickory set out a week later with twenty-five hundred men.

The army moved quickly — *too* quickly for the civilian contractors hired to deliver supplies. As a result, the advance into Creek country became a living nightmare. Men trudged through knee-deep mud; nettles stung bare skin, raising rows of red welts. Empty stomachs gurgled. The troops lived on roots, berries, even the bark of trees. Jackson had the army's few cattle butchered, taking for himself and the officers the brains, intestines, and other waste parts, which they ate without salt; the best cuts went to the common soldiers.

It wasn't enough. Grumbling spread through the ranks, mainly among the newer companies, which hadn't learned respect, or fear, for the general. A private stood in front of Jackson, shouting into his face for something to eat. "I will divide what I have with you," Old Hickory replied, offering a handful of acorns. The man stepped back into the ranks without another word.

Jackson could put up with grumbling, because he knew how the men felt. Disobedience, however, was another matter. One day several companies refused to go any further. They had enlisted to fight Indians, they said, not to starve or walk their legs off. They were going home, General Jackson or not. That was mutiny.

Old Hickory's face flushed scarlet, and it took every ounce of self-control to keep from rushing among the mutineers with his sword. Instead, he grabbed a musket from a soldier and rode into their path. Resting the gun-barrel across the horse's neck, he swore to shoot the first man who moved toward him. His shoulder ached, and pain was etched on his face, but the mutineers knew he meant business. After some tense moments, they moved off in the right direction. Jackson returned the musket, only to be told that it was broken and couldn't fire.

Another time, Jackson heard a soldier threaten an officer. "Shoot him! Shoot him!" he screamed in his high-pitched voice, charging out of his tent. After a court-martial, the man was shot at sunrise before the whole army. No wonder rumor had it that Jackson's troops feared him more than the enemy.

Tough as he was, Jackson suffered worse than anyone in the ranks. In addition to his throbbing shoulder, he came down with dysentery, an uncontrollable form of diarrhea that sent stabbing cramps through his stomach. And he was lonely — lonelier than he'd been since his mother's death. He missed Rachel and little Andrew. "Kiss him for his papa," he wrote her, "and give him nuts and ginger cake."

Jackson's army met and defeated the Creeks at places with tongue-twister names like Emuckfau, Tallassahatche, and Econochaca. Finally, at the end of March, 1814, he stood before the Creeks' main stronghold. They had built a large village at the Horseshoe Bend of the Tallapoosa River in northeastern Alabama. The river's loop was a natural fortress, protected on three sides by water. The fourth, or landward, side was guarded by a fortification of heavy logs. And, for good measure, hundreds of canoes were tied along the riverbank for a quick getaway if necessary.

While some of John Coffee's men swam the river to cut the canoes' ropes, setting them adrift, Jackson's infantry and artillery pounded the Indians' defense line. The battle raged all day, as the desperate braves vowed to die fighting.

Their determination forced the general to order a frontal assault. His infantry charged the barricade, ignoring the

Jackson threatened to shoot any man who wouldn't go forward during his campaign against the Creek Indians. He later learned that the musket he aimed was broken and wouldn't fire.

dead and wounded who fell out of line. The first man over the barricade was Ensign Sam Houston; one day he'd be President of the Texas Republic. The braves fought on, hoping only to take more soldiers with them before they died. "We shot them like dogs," said Davy Crockett, who'd be killed one day at the Alamo fighting for Texas independence. The bodies of nearly nine hundred Indians and forty-seven whites littered the battlefield. Fort Mims had been avenged.

Among the prisoners was a three-year-old boy not unlike the child at the Hermitage. His parents were dead and he looked lonely and frightened. Using his good hand, Old Hickory dissolved some brown sugar in water and coaxed the child to drink. He then sent him to live with an Alabama family at his own expense.

Jackson was reunited with his family only a short time when a dust-covered rider reined in his horse at the Hermitage. He brought urgent news from the War Department: Jackson had been promoted to major general in the regular United States Army and put in command of all forces in the South. He'd need every ounce of toughness for his new assignment.

Disturbing news was coming from the Gulf of Mexico. British warships seemed bolder than usual. Hit-and-run raids along the coast were increasing. Spies reported feverish activity at the British base of Negril Bay, Jamaica. Something was in the wind, something important. The last and most dangerous part of Britain's master plan was getting underway.

Acting on a hunch, Jackson rushed troops and heavy guns to old Fort Bowyer at the entrance to Mobile Bay. Mobile's deep-water harbor was a perfect staging area for a drive inland, and he didn't want to be caught off guard at such a vital spot. His hunch paid off a few weeks later, when the fort's garrison drove off a British landing force, destroying one man-of-war and killing nearly two hundred of the Redcoats.

That landing force had come from Pensacola fifty miles to the East. Spanish neutrality in Florida was a sham. At the very moment the Spanish government spoke of friendship with the United States, the British flag flew over one of Pensacola's forts. British warships rode at anchor in the harbor. Redcoats drilled Indians before sending them to raid American settlements.

General Jackson now made good use of the skills of Judge Jackson. His orders from Washington were clear on one point: they said the government didn't want war with Spain and advised him not to invade Florida. *Advised*, not commanded. Well, he reasoned, nobody could accuse him of disobedience if he ignored the advice and went after the enemy.

Before fighting, however, he decided to try diplomacy for the last time. Writing to the Spanish governor, he explained that he couldn't allow the British to launch attacks from the safety of neutral territory. The letter ended with a phrase only a fool could misunderstand: "An Eye for an Eye, Tooth for Tooth, and Scalp for Scalp."

The governor misunderstood. When he pooh-poohed the threat, Old Hickory stormed into Florida at the head of three thousand troops, arriving at Pensacola on the afternoon of November 7, 1814. Before the defenders realized what was happening, John Coffee's horsemen were whooping and firing their pistols in the streets. The Spaniards surrendered. Their British friends blew up their fort, boarded their ships, and escaped. The governor offered to kiss the conqueror's hands, but the stony-faced man with the scarecrow legs had no time for such nonsense.

The more Old Hickory thought about the British actions, the more he became convinced that Mobile and Pensacola were sideshows. There was no time to lose now. Jackson marched his army back to Mobile at double quick time and, after further strengthening its defenses, hurried to New Orleans. That's where the enemy would strike next.

Four days after Jackson left Mobile, November 26, 1814, a British invasion fleet sailed from Jamaica. The fleet stretched for miles across the blue Caribbean. Admiral Cochrane, commanding, led the way in the eighty-gun *Tonnant*, followed by five seventy-four-gun ships-of-the-line and fifty-four other vessels. Aboard the ships were fourteen thousand troops, the pick of the British Army. In addition to the regiments that burned Washington, there were combat-tested units from Europe, including the Ninety-third Highlanders complete with kilts and bagpipes. Marines, artillerymen, engineers, rocketeers, and two Negro regiments from the West Indies rounded out the assault force.

Major General the Honorable Sir Edward Packenham led the army. At thirty-seven, this nobleman was hero of scores of battles against Napoleon. His teacher in the art of war was his brother-in-law, the "Iron" Duke of Wellington, the British Army's leading commander. Packenham's force was so large that he needed three other major generals as assistants: John Keane, Sir Samuel Gibbs, John Lambert. The fleet carried civilians as well as soldiers. There were hundreds of government officials and tax collectors, printers and secretaries — everyone needed to set up a new colony. The army officers brought their wives along for company and to lend a feeling of home in the wilds of North America. Nobody aboard that magnificent fleet doubted that the ladies would need their silk gowns for the victory ball in New Orleans.

Old Hickory found New Orleans wide open to attack. Studying the map, he saw that an enemy had several lines of approach. The city, which was part of President Jefferson's Louisiana Purchase from France, lies on the left bank of the Mississippi River, about a hundred miles from its mouth. The country in between is mostly swamps that used to teem with alligators, muskrats, and birds of every kind from delicate flamingoes to clumsy-looking pelicans. A maze of winding, muddy waterways, called bayous, laces the countryside. An army that found the right bayou could advance to the gates of New Orleans without being seen until it was too late. An army that lost its way in the bayous would be food for alligators and leeches. Finally, there is Lake Borgne, a wide, shallow bay that sweeps to within six miles of the Mississippi below the city.

Jackson sealed off each of these attack routes. Fort Bourbon and Fort St. Philip on the Mississippi were strengthened with heavy artillery positioned to catch invading ships in a crossfire. Teams of woodcutters sent trees crashing across bayous to form jackstraw tangles that would take weeks to clear. A squadron of five gunboats began patrolling Lake Borgne. Their job was not to engage the enemy but warn the general of his approach.

In the meantime Old Hickory collected as strange an assortment of troops as ever served under the Stars and Stripes. Among them were Creoles, people of French ancestry born in Louisiana, dressed in gaudy uniforms of red, blue, and gold. There were also many Frenchmen who had served in Napoleon's armies and were a match for any

Redcoat. Choctaw Indians led by Chief Push-Ma-Ta-Ha served in the ranks, along with hundreds of "Free Men of Color," free Negroes from Santo Domingo in the West Indies. When it came to fighting men, the general was color blind; he didn't care how his soldiers looked so long as they could handle their weapons. A paymaster received the tonguelashing of his life for holding back the wages of nonwhites. Wages were to be paid promptly, said Jackson in his nastiest tones, "without inquiring whether the troops are white, black, or tea."

The army even had room for outlaws. The Lafitte brothers, Jean and Pierre, led a pirate band that specialized in capturing Spanish ships and smuggling. The British had promised the Lafittes money if they'd join them, but the brothers offered their services to the Americans instead. Jackson, however, refused to deal with these "hellish banditti" until Jean, the elder brother and head of the band, strolled into his headquarters. We don't know what they said in private, but they must have gotten along well, for Old Hickory never said another harsh word about the pirates.

The backbone of the American forces were the *Kaintucks*. A Kaintuck wasn't necessarily from Kentucky, but anyone who had come from the wild country upriver. The genteel New Orleanaise turned up their noses at these backwoodsmen. Their dress certainly wasn't the height of fashion: deerskin or homespun clothes dyed with berries and hats of raccoon or fox, tails and all. As for cleanliness, well, Kaintucks dunked in a rain barrel once a month whether they needed a bath or not. Otherwise, their greasy hair hung like a shaggy mane around their shoulders. They stank so badly that townbred people couldn't stand to be downwind of them. They crawled with fleas. And they drank. It was said that a Kaintuck would sooner go hungry than do without his whiskey bottle. Not that they were drunkards, but whiskey warmed their insides during the dank, cold winters, and there was nothing like it for aching bones and rotting teeth.

Sober or drunk, the Kaintuck was a dangerous fellow, a walking arsenal. Scalping knives and a tomahawk bristled

The Gulf of Mexico Front and the Area Around New Orleans

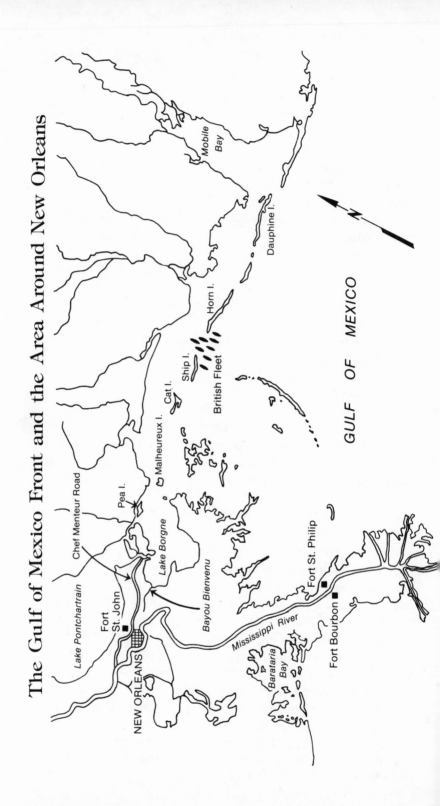

Mobile Bay

Dauphine I.

Horn I.

Ship I.

British Fleet

Malheureux I.

Cat I.

Chef Menteur Road

Pea I.

Lake Pontchartrain

Fort St. John

Lake Borgne

Bayou Bienvenu

NEW ORLEANS

Mississippi River

Fort St. Philip

Barataria Bay

Fort Bourbon

GULF   OF   MEXICO

from his belt, while a sheath with a wicked-looking hunting knife was tucked into his boot. But his most fearsome weapon was the Kentucky long rifle. The regular army soldier was a musketeer, the Kaintuck a rifleman. The two weapons are quite different. The musket was an inaccurate, short-range weapon. The rifle, however, had an extra-long barrel into which spiral grooves (riflings) were cut so that the bullet would spin in flight. Spinning gave the bullet greater range and accuracy, in the same way that a quarterback puts a spin on the football when throwing long passes. The Kentucky long rifle could outreach any musket by a hundred yards. To make it even deadlier, the Kaintucks fired "buck and ball," two small buckshots in addition to the normal bullet.

The day of battle was nearer than Old Hickory believed. He still thought he had several weeks to prepare when the British fleet anchored outside Lake Borgne, December 14, 1814. Since the lake was too shallow for men-of-war, Admiral Cochrane sent a swarm of barges armed with carronades to knock out the American gunboats. After rowing steadily for a full day, the British invaders found the gunboats becalmed, unable to use their sails. During the battle that followed, British boarders captured the gunboats and their crews. Not a man escaped to tell Jackson that the enemy had forced open a main approach to New Orleans.

Admiral Cochrane did his best during the following week to keep the fleet out of sight while patrols searched for a way through the swamps. Bayou after bayou was explored, only to be found choked with fallen trees. Officers were beginning to lose hope when a patrol found a completely clear bayou. Its name was Bayou Bienvenue — Bayou Welcome — and the British welcomed it as a gift from Heaven. To this day we don't know why it was overlooked by Jackson's axemen.

On the morning of December 23, 1814, General Keane's eighteen-hundred-man advance force rowed across Lake Borgne and into the bayou. Upon touching solid ground several hours later, the troops fanned out behind a clump of

British barges attack American gunboats becalmed on Lake Borgne. Their victory was so swift and so complete that Jackson didn't know the enemy was in the area until several days later.

trees. Across a clearing they saw a sugar plantation owned by a Creole family named Villeré.

Nothing stirred, not even a bird. On the porch of the plantation house sat the owner's son, Major Gabriel Villeré of the Louisiana militia. His feet rested on the porch railing and he took long, easy puffs on a Spanish cigar. It tasted

good until, looking up, he found himself ringed with bayonets. Redcoats were pouring out of the woods. While some set up a command post in the house, others took up positions along the river a few hundred yards away.

Major Villeré was scared, not for himself, but for New Orleans. Somehow he had to warn Jackson of the enemy's presence a mere seven miles from the city. With Redcoats all about, he leaped through a closed window and ran for the swamp. Bullets whined overhead, but he kept going. Crossing the river, he borrowed a horse and rode away at breakneck speed.

The British might still have won had they moved quickly. A two-hour march would have brought them to their goal before Old Hickory could organize a counterattack. But General Keane hesitated. His men were tired and hungry, having gone without a hot meal for days. Keane decided to wait at the plantation for Sir Edward Packenham to take charge. In waiting, he threw away a golden opportunity that would never return.

Major Villeré poured out a torrent of French that none of the American officers understood. As another Creole translated, Jackson's lips pressed together tightly, turning white. The scar on his forehead whitened. "By the Eternal," he thundered, unable to control himself, "they shall not sleep on our soil!"

His temper cooled a moment later. Already a plan was forming in his mind. "Gentlemen," he declared, turning to his aides, "the British are below. We must fight them tonight." Some had already left the room when he slowly ground his fist into the palm of his hand. "I will smash them, so help me God!" he mumbled to himself.

Messengers tore through the streets of New Orleans. Church bells clanged. Drums beat the call to assembly. At three o'clock in the afternoon, exactly an hour after Major Villeré's arrival, Old Hickory set out with eighteen hundred men, to be followed next day by the bulk of the army. The armed schooner *Carolina* slipped her cable and silently glided downstream to support the infantry.

It was pitch dark at 6:30 P.M. when the Americans took up attack positions. No one spoke above a whisper. A mist had settled over the Mississippi, so that the only light came from British campfires. Even if Major Villeré got through, General Keane was sure it would take the Americans at least a day to mount a counterattack. Tonight, surely, was safe, he thought, for not even a fire-eater like Jackson would risk hitting his own men in the darkness.

The Redcoats had just lay down to sleep when the ghostly shadow of *Carolina* loomed over the riverbank. "Now, then," they heard a voice cry, "give it to them for the honor of America!" The guns roared, belching fire and smoke, sending troops diving for cover as iron balls plowed the campsite. Brave men risked their lives to throw water on the campfires; sometimes they threw themselves on the fires to put them out quickly.

Jackson let the bombardment continue for a half hour. Then, with every eye turned toward the ship, he ordered the infantry to charge the enemy's flank. A furious, no-hold-barred fight erupted in the darkness. Men shot not at each other, but at gunflashes across the way. Men rolled on the ground, hands wrapped around each other's throat. Hunting knives found their mark.

The Redcoats were surprised but, like true professionals, kept their wits. Gradually the sergeants rallied their squads. "Charge! Charge! Push on the bayonet!" they shouted. The action swayed back and forth until midnight, when Jackson gave the signal to withdraw. American losses were two hundred seventeen killed, wounded and captured, compared to two hundred seventy-seven for the British.

Yet this first skirmish in the battle for New Orleans was far from a draw. It was the beginning of the end for the invaders. For while Keane held the battlefield, Jackson pulled back a few miles to the Rodriguez Canal, a dry drainage ditch ten feet wide and four feet deep. The army halted thirty yards behind this ditch and began to dig. Work went on throughout the night in almost total darkness. As one rank slept on its weapons, the other dug with pick and shovel, bayonet and bare hands. Only the general stayed on duty the whole night. He never left the line, never slept.

At sunrise the British saw a rough breastwork of mud and earth looming in their path. Three-quarters of a mile long, it stretched from an impassable swamp straight down to the Mississippi River. Old Hickory had drawn the line.

If the invaders wanted New Orleans, they'd have to go past him to get it.

General Packenham arrived with strong reinforcements on Christmas Day, 1814. The experienced officer sized up the situation immediately. The key, it seemed, lay with the *Carolina* and the newly-arrived *Louisiana*. As long as these vessels stood offshore to rake his lines, it would be impossible to attack Jackson's breastwork.

Working under cover of darkness, the British placed several small-caliber cannon along the riverbank. At dawn, December 27, red-hot balls were lifted out of their furnaces and dropped down the gun barrels. *Carolina*, her crew taken by surprise, was riddled with hot shot. Luckily, a quick-thinking officer ordered "Abandon Ship" moments before the magazine exploded with a noise that rattled windows in New Orleans.

The British gunners cheered as they turned their attention to the *Louisiana*. Just then the wind died down, forcing the crew to scramble into the longboats to pull her upriver. Slowly, with cannonballs bouncing across *Louisiana*'s deck, they rowed her out of range.

Despite the loss of a ship, Jackson's line grew stronger by the hour. Every man, shovel, and weapon that could be spared from New Orleans was rushed to the breastwork. Two thousand Negro laborers, half of them slaves, toiled around the clock to strengthen the lines. One artillery position was manned by red-shirted pirates commanded by Dominique You, the Lafittes' trusted lieutenant. On sea or land, the pirates knew how to handle cannon, and the bigger the better.

Packenham launched his first large-scale assault the next day, December 28. The attack began with an artillery bombardment and masses of Congreve rockets. The Americans grew restless, since few had ever seen "the rockets' red glare." Old Hickory rode along the line on a white horse, encouraging the men by his own example. Luckily, the British had no Kaintucks in their ranks, for he made a perfect target for a long rifle. Cheers followed him down the line. "Don't mind these rockets," he shouted, waving his hat. "They are mere toys to amuse children." The cheers turned to laughter as the rockets passed overhead harmlessly.

Next came the British infantry, no laughing matter. They came forward in long, dense columns, a moving wall of humanity. Bugles blew, sounding commands to dress the lines, or increase the pace, or move right or left. The bagpipes of the Ninety-third Highlanders sounded their mournful tune, as if the instruments themselves longed for the green hills of home. Bayonets glistened in the sunlight.

As the columns advanced, *Louisiana* peppered their flank with grape shot. Guns on the breastwork began throw-

Jackson rode a white horse in the front line during the Battle of New Orleans.

ing heavier shot. Riflemen spat a last stream of chewing tobacco before taking aim.

Redcoats were already dropping when Packenham realized the attack would fail. Rather than waste his men's lives, he called back the columns. He had been disappointed for the second time in as many days. There would be no third setback, he vowed. Next time he'd punch a hole in the American breastwork wide enough for the columns to sweep through without breaking ranks.

The British spent the following days hauling guns from the fleet through Bayou Bienvenue to the front line. These were not the popguns that had demolished *Carolina*, but eighteen- and twenty-four-pound naval guns — ship killers. Thirty guns were brought up and, to strengthen their emplacements, huge barrels called hogsheads, filled with sugar, formed into a breastwork.

On New Year's Day, 1815, the Americans were treated to the greatest (until then) bombardment in the nation's history. It came as a total surprise. The area was shrouded in fog as Jackson's army prepared to greet the New Year with a parade followed by a hearty meal sent as a gift from the people of New Orleans. The general himself was dressing for the festivities at headquarters, a nearby plantation house. He didn't feel especially happy about the New Year. His dysentery had become worse, and boiled rice was the only food his stomach could hold down. The pain was so severe that he had to bend over with his chest pressed against a piece of furniture until the cramps stopped. He looked like a living skeleton in a baggy uniform.

The British cannon boomed all together. Rockets screeched overhead. Jackson watched the barrage from a top-floor window until splintering glass and falling plaster made him decide that it was safer with the troops in the front line. Over a hundred shots hit the house in ten minutes.

The British, however, quickly lost the advantage of surprise. Although they wrecked three American cannon and blew up an ammunition wagon, the gunners were too hungry and exhausted from the night's work to aim carefully. Most of their shot flew harmlessly over the Americans' heads.

Jackson's "Dirty Shirts," as the British called frontiersmen, began to find the enemy's range. Within fifteen minutes they were tearing the enemy positions to pieces. One after another their guns were dismounted and the crews killed. Splinters from shattered hogsheads flew about crazily. The unrefined sugar spilled out of the barrels and, mixing with the light rain that began to fall, became a black, sticky soup. The hungry soldiers scooped up the sugar and ate it from cupped hands, making them violently sick. Between the cries of the wounded, the noise of the guns, and the smell of gunsmoke and vomit, the British position seemed like hell. Sir Edward Packenham had failed again.

That failure made him pause to rethink the situation. Two things were now certain. First, Jackson's breastworks could not be taken by head-on assault. Secondly, the swamp and Mississippi River at either end of the American line prevented flank attacks. Yet there *was* a weak point — across the river, where only several hundred militiamen stood guard.

Packenham's new plan was so simple that he scolded himself for not having thought of it earlier. He would send part of his army across the river in rowboats to drive off the militia and capture their twelve heavy guns. As the main attack moved toward Jackson's breastwork, these troops would pound his right flank with the captured guns. Pressed from front and side, the Americans would have to give up the Rodriguez Canal defense line. They'd probably keep running until they reached New Orleans.

But Old Hickory was not to be taken by surprise again. Night patrols were sent to watch the enemy and report any unusual activity. They had plenty to report. On the night of January 7, 1815, they heard troop movements along the whole British line. Flat-bottomed boats were seen being hauled overland and refloated in the Mississippi.

Jackson was asleep when, toward midnight, an officer arrived with the latest report. He walked gingerly across the darkened room, trying not to step on the general's aides, who were sleeping on the floor around his cot.

Old Hickory nodded as he listened to the whispered message. "Gentlemen," he said softly, almost kindly, "we have slept enough." The final battle of the War of 1812 was about to begin.

The whole army was soon astir, checking equipment and eating an early breakfast, usually a chunk of corn bread washed down with whiskey. "It's the general!" men whispered in hushed tones as Old Hickory visited each unit.

He had a good word for everyone. The pirates, good Frenchmen that they were, needed coffee to start the day. "That smells like better coffee than we can get," said Jackson, glancing at Dominique You. "Smuggle it?" The fierce little man smiled and, filling the general's cup, answered, "Mebbe so, *Géneral.*"

Jackson visited each group in turn, assuring them that the day would go well. His warmest greetings were for his own Tennesseans. They crowded around him in the gloom, and he called out names by the sound of voices.

"Joe, how are they using you?" he said to a Nashville teenager. "Wouldn't you rather be with Aunt Lucy than with me?"

"Not by a damned sight, General," came the reply.

"Stick to 'em, Joe." He clapped the private on the back and moved on. Altogether Jackson had 5,172 men in the line, with not an inch of standing room to spare for another.

Dawn, January 8, 1815. A rocket rose from the British lines, hung in the air, and burst into a silver-blue shower. Moments later, an answering rocket came from the riverbank. "That's their signal to advance, I believe," said Jackson. It was indeed.

The sun burned off the last patches of fog, revealing an awesome sight. British regiments were moving across the plain in solid columns. They came on silently, without drumbeat or bugle call, in files so straight that they could have been aligned with a ruler.

At first the Americans could only stare at the red waves. Then, either for joy or to relieve the tension, the Tennesseans began to cheer. The Kentuckians, not to be outdone, took up the cry.

These frontiersmen were confident as they stood behind their breastwork. A backwoods poet later captured their mood in a song, *The Hunters of Kentucky*:

> Behind it stood our little force —
> None wished it to be greater;
> For ev'ry man was half a horse,
> And half an alligator.

Jackson watched the Redcoats marching behind their hedge of bayonets. A mile away. Half a mile. Old Hickory nodded and the band struck up *Yankee Doodle*, which would blare out, over and over again, until the battle ended.

Jackson nodded again, and the artillery began to tune up. The first shots scattered, as the gunners tested the range. Then an earthshaking roar erupted from the American line. Redcoated bodies and parts of bodies flew into the air like store window dummies in a tornado.

Openings appeared in the oncoming ranks, but were quickly filled. "Close up! Close up!" the sergeants cried. The Redcoats obeyed; they were taught to ignore the fallen as so many colorful logs. They stepped over the bodies without breaking formation.

Each Kaintuck rifleman pressed his cheek against his weapon's wooden stock and sighted down the long barrel. His target was the metal plate over the spot where the white belts crossed on a Redcoat's chest.

Jackson raised his sword, bringing it down with a sharp, slashing motion.

"Fire!"

Sheets of orange flame lashed out from the breastwork. The crowded riflemen fired so rapidly that they seemed not to be reloading.

The British front crumpled. Redcoats didn't fall singly, but in batches. Entire companies toppled over as if felled by an enormous scythe. Deafened by noise, blinded by smoke, the advancing ranks began to trip over the fallen. Then it happened. The Americans found themselves staring

A bird's-eye view of the Battle of New Orleans. The British columns along the bottom and at the right are being mowed down by the tightly packed American riflemen and gunners on the left.

in disbelief at one of the rarest sights in warfare: British regulars broke ranks and began to flee in panic.

Packenham was with General Gibbs' column on the American left when the troops broke. "For shame!" he shouted. "Remember that you are British soldiers. *This* is the road you ought to take."

No one, British or American, had greater personal courage than this officer. Taking off his hat, he placed it on the point of his sword and ran forward. The soldiers, seeing their general out front, rallied to the attack. It was useless. Packenham, his arm already broken by a bullet, toppled over with bullets through the legs and stomach. Moments after, Gibbs received a mortal wound, dying the next day. The renewed attack fell apart.

Yet the battle was far from over. The Ninety-third Highlanders made straight for the American center. They were proud men, handsome men, none shorter than six feet. They marched in tight-packed ranks, heads high, staring straight ahead. Their bagpipes struck up a marching tune, whose high-pitched wail nearly drowned out *Yankee Doodle.* The Yankee riflemen chopped them down like grass before a lawnmower.

General Keane's column fared no better along the river. The general and half his men fell in front of a withering fire within a few minutes. A handful of soldiers, however, managed to reach the Rodriguez Canal. Major Wilkinson crossed the canal and mounted the breastwork beyond, shouting "Hurrah, boys, the day is our own! Why don't the troops follow?" There were no troops to follow. His brave handful were lying dead in the canal. As he called to them the riflemen shot him too.

Another officer, Lieutenant Lavack, mounted the breastwork. Sword in hand, he demanded that the Americans surrender. An officer pointed a finger, indicating that Lavack should look over his shoulder. He turned and was astonished to find himself alone. He alone, of all his men, had survived, only to become a prisoner.

The Redcoats' only success was across the river, where they easily overran the undermanned defenses. The Americans retreated, spiking their guns to make them useless.*

Yet Jackson's fear that the British would move upstream to capture New Orleans quickly passed. General Lambert, the highest surviving enemy officer, was shocked at the heaps of bodies on the ground. Enough was enough. He ordered a retreat, halting the slaughter.

The victorious Americans were also shocked at the sight of the battlefield. One could have walked a quarter-mile from their breastwork on British bodies. The enemy

---

* "Spiking" means to hammer a heavy iron spike so tightly into a cannon's touchhole that the match can't set off the powder charge.

had lost 2,036 killed and wounded, plus five hundred prisoners — half his total combat strength. Of the nine hundred who marched with the Highlanders, only one hundred and sixty dazed, bleeding men survived after seven minutes of battle. American losses were seven killed and six wounded. Old Hickory, who wasn't a religious man, could only say that the hand of God had shielded his boys.

The real tragedy of the Battle of New Orleans only became known weeks later. The battle had been a mistake — a horrible, bloody mistake. For on December 24, 1814, American and British diplomats met at Ghent, Belgium, to sign a treaty ending the War of 1812. The final and greatest battle of the war was unnecessary. Hundreds died and thousands were wounded simply because people in the early nineteenth century lacked the means of instantaneous communication available today.

What makes the Peace of Christmas Eve doubly ironic is that it said nothing about the grievances that had caused the war. It wasn't necessary to mention them. The defeat of Napoleon ended the British blockade of France, and with it the reason for impressing seamen and searching neutral ships. French defeat, not American victory, made a reality of the slogan "Free Trade and Sailors' Rights." The death of Tecumseh, moreover, broke the back of Indian resistance in the Old Northwest. American settlers soon flocked into the area; with so much land available so cheaply, or at no cost at all, the War Hawks' dream of a Canadian empire was forgotten.

The peacemakers at Ghent signed a treaty that turned the clock back to June, 1812. Neither side gained nor lost territory. Thus the War of 1812 really was The War Nobody Won.

Old Hickory, of course, didn't know this until weeks after the Battle of New Orleans. All he knew was that he had won a magnificent victory and avenged his scar.

Yet he wasn't boastful or loud in self-praise. He missed Rachel and little Andrew, missed them bitterly. But he missed his mother most of all. During quiet moments with his aides, his thoughts drifted back over the years to that strong, wise lady. He told them how she'd risked her life nursing prisoners during the Revolution. And he recited the lessons of her farewell letter. Be brave. Be truthful. Be loyal. Respect yourself and stand up for your rights. "Gentlemen, those words have been the law of my life."

Pointless as it may seem today, the War of 1812 was a milestone in our nation's history. Its boldest military leaders eventually became peacetime leaders: Jackson and William Henry Harrison as our seventh and ninth presidents; Richard Johnson, who led the charge against Tecumseh, as vice-president in the 1830s.

Peace also brought the healing of wounds and understanding between former enemies. By the end of the nineteenth century, the United States and Canada shared the longest demilitarized border in the world. By the twentieth century, British-American friendship had become so firm that they fought as allies in two world wars.

*   *   *

The last word, however, belongs to two members of Parliament, overheard after a debate over a dispute with the United States in 1829:

"We had better yield a point or two than go to war with the Americans," said the first.

"Yes," replied the second. "We shall get nothing but hard knocks there."

Maybe that conversation expressed the most important outcome of The War Nobody Won. For at last the Mother Country understood that the United States was a true nation and not merely a breakaway colony. At last the young republic could take its rightful place among the family of nations.

Some More Books

Chidsey, Donald B. *The Battle of New Orleans.* New York: Crown Publishers, 1968.

Cleaves, Freeman. *Old Tippecanoe: William Henry Harrison and His times.* Port Washington, New York: Kennikat Press, 1969.

Coles, Harry L. *The War of 1812.* University of Chicago Press, 1965.

Dillon, Richard. *We Have Met the Enemy: Oliver Hazard Perry, Wilderness Commander.* New York: McGraw-Hill Book Company, 1978.

Dutton, Charles J. *Oliver Hazard Perry.* New York: Longman, Green and Company, 1935.

Forester, C. S. *The Age of Fighting Sail: The Story of the Naval War of 1812.* Garden City, New York: Doubleday, 1956.

James, Marquis. *Andrew Jackson, the Border Captain.* New York: Garden City Publishing Company, 1940.

Kraft, Herman F. and Norris, Walter B. *Sea Power in American History.* New York: The Century Company, 1923.

Muller, Charles G. *The Darkest Day: 1814, The Washington-Baltimore Campaign.* Philadelphia: J. B. Lippincott Company, 1963.

Pratt, Fletcher. *The Heroic Years: Fourteen Years of the Republic, 1801–1815.* New York: Smith and Haas, 1934.

———— *The Navy: A History.* Garden City, New York: Doubleday, 1938.

Pullen, H. F. *The Shannon and the Chesapeake.* Toronto: McClelland and Stewart, Ltd., 1970.

Rothberg, Gunther E. *The Art of War in the Age of Napoleon.* Bloomington, Indiana: Indiana University Press, 1980.

Tucker, Glenn. *Poltroons and Patriots: A Popular Account of the War of 1812.* Indianapolis: The Bobbs-Merrill Co., 2 volumes, 1954.

———— *Tecumseh: The Vision of Glory.* New York: Russell and Russell, 1973.

Tully, Andrew. *When We Burned the White House.* New York: Simon and Schuster, 1961.

Williams, T. Harry. *The History of American Wars: From Colonial Times to World War I.* New York: Alfred A. Knopf, 1981.

Index

171

British: *Detroit*, 85, 86, 87,
88, 89, 90, 91, 95;
Devastation, 131; *Erebus*,
133; HMS *Leopard*,
attacks USS *Chesapeake*,
36, 71; HMS *Macedonian*,
defeated by USS *United
States*, 64-69; *Meteor*,
131; *Queen Charlotte*, 88,
95; HMS *Shannon*,
defeats USS *Chesapeake*,
70-73; *Terror*, 131;
Volcano, 133
ships-of-the-line, 43
Skinner, Colonel John, 133
sloops of war, 45
Smith, General Samuel, 129
Stricker, General John, 130
Stuart, Gilbert, 118
Suter, Mrs. Barbara, 122

Tecumseh, Shawnee chief, 16-
18, 25, 27, 29, 37, 38,
39, 40, 87, 97, 98, 99,
101-102, 168
Thames River, battle, 99-103
Tippecanoe, battle of, 19, 37
Trafalgar, battle of, 6, 11, 51,
85, 126

United States Army
strength, 21; uniforms, 22;
weapons, 23; medical
service, 24

United States Capitol, 115,
120-123
United States Navy
size and strength, 52

Villerè, Major Gabriel, 154-
156

War Hawks, 16, 19, 104
War of 1812
causes, 10-19; Indian raids
as a cause, 15-18;
opposition to "Mr.
Madison's War," 20; ends,
167; results, 167-168
Washington, D.C.
British plans to capture city,
107; appearance in 1814,
115-116, 125
Wellington, Duke of, 149
White House (President's
House), 115-117; burned
by British, 122
Wilson, Samuel ("Uncle
Sam"), 33
Winchester, General James, 34
Winder, General William, 111,
112

Yarnell, Lieutenant John D., 92
York (Toronto), 97
You, Dominique, 158, 162

PICTURE CREDITS